Reformation
Anglicanism

Biblical – Generous – Beautiful

Forward by Ashley Null

Chuck Collins

Anglican House
Publishers

Published by Anglican House Publishers, Inc., Newport Beach, California. You may contact us at http://www.ahpub.org Text set in Optima typeface. Printed by Asia Printing Co., Ltd., Seoul, Korea.

Scripture quotations are from the New Revised Standard Version Bible, copyright © 1989 the Division of Christian Education of the National Council of the Churches of Christ in the United States of America. Used by permission. All rights reserved.

ANGLICAN HOUSE
PUBLISHERS

ISBN: 978-0-9860441-4-4

The Most Rev. Foley Beach (Archbishop and Primate, Anglican Church in North America)

"Chuck Collins gives a clear and concise explanation of the story of Anglicanism from its early roots to its modern day relevance. *Reformational Anglicanism* is not only informative, but it is inspirational to see how God has used this expression of the Christian Faith to impact the world for Jesus Christ."

The Rev. Dr. J. I. Packer (Author and Theologian)

"This lively and enlivening introduction to real Anglicanism speaks loud and clear to those who want to be serious with the Bible and its God. It is a forthright recall to the things that really matter."

The Very Rev. Dr. Justyn Terry (Dean President, Trinity School for Ministry)

"Dear Chuck, I have very much enjoyed reading your book. I also remember reading the earlier edition and using it to lead a woman to Christ at Dallas/Fort Worth airport... With so many people discovering Anglicanism at the moment there is a great need for well-informed and clearly written accounts of this great tradition. Chuck Collins provides just that. He is able to explain the main points of Anglicanism and show their consistency with Protestant convictions with the lightness of touch of an experienced pastor. It is a joy to read and I recommend it highly."

iii

The Rt. Rev. Dr. Felix Orji (ACNA Bishop)

"There is significant confusion today as to what Anglicanism is. To God's glory and the blessing of his Church, Venerable Chuck Collins has succinctly and in a timely fashion clarified for us what Anglicanism is and ought to be --- a church that is Scriptural, Reformational and ordered. I highly recommend it to the church."

The Most Rev. Dr. Paul Zahl (Author and Theologian)

"Although I write as one who decided to stay within the Episcopal Church, I think Chuck Collins has given us a simple, succinct, and completely accessible picture of the religion that Anglicanism seeks to be. If you are looking for a religious way of life that is beautiful, is anchored in centuries of wisdom and pastoral caring, and at the same time has meat on its bones, Walk Right In! "Collins' book, like Thomas Cranmer's Church, has wide open doors for any person who is making their Pilgrim's Progress towards a safe enduring Home."

The Rev. Canon David H. Roseberry (Rector, Christ Church Plano)

"Chuck Collins has traced the history and practice of a group of believers that form the largest protestant denomination in the world. It is a formidable task, to be sure. But it is a great story…full of twists, turns, tumbles, and turnovers. We are in one of those times right now. However, the Lord continues to draw people to this church. So read this chronicle of our history and rejoice that God continues to call and inspire Anglicans in America...and then join us...or invite someone to join you in the Anglican Way."

The Very Rev. Kevin Martin (Retired Dean, St. Matthew's Episcopal Cathedral, Dallas)

"Chuck Collins has written a very useful book on the nature of Anglicanism. This work establishes the historic roots and doctrinal underpinning of true Anglicanism. He handles the differences among Anglicans in North America in a fair handed way. Those of us interested in the future reconciliation and growth of Anglicanism in North America will find this a helpful tool in that direction. It will also serve as a good introduction to the Anglican faith and spirituality to those new to our tradition."

Forward

Softly and tenderly Jesus is calling
Calling for you and for me;
See, on the portals He's waiting and watching
Watching for you and for me.

Come Home, come home,
Ye who are weary, come home;
Earnestly, tenderly, Jesus is calling,
Calling, O sinner, come home!

Growing up in the Episcopal Church I did not encounter this famous invitation hymn of the Moody Revivals until I watched Horton Foote's *The Trip to Bountiful*. In this wonderful story, an elderly woman manages to escape from the cramped urban apartment she shares with her over-protective son and bossy daughter-in-law to go back just once more to her hometown of Bountiful, Texas. Experiencing her greatest joys but mingled as well with her deepest heartbreaks, in Bountiful she had felt the most alive. Now, past memory, personal meaning and future hope all seem tightly bound up and tied down to that specific soil which her family had tilled and which had covered her two children dying in an undue season. Realizing that Jesus would soon be calling her home to Heaven, Mrs. Watts needs to get her bearings for her final journey by one last trip to the place and time that had given coherence to her life on earth. She has to feel the earth of the home place run through her fingers once again and remember the person she was before cramped relationships in that Houston apartment had turned her bitter and despondent. Only remembering the truths about herself and others from that earlier time can she come home to her own gentle, tender, earnest self.

In the midst of all the turmoil, division, heartbreak and bitterness of North American Anglicanism in the Twenty-first Century, Chuck Collins has written a lively and informative book that asks his readers to go on a similar journey to the past in order to recover our true loving selves for the future. To old Episcopalians and newly minted Anglicans, Chuck reminds them of their long mutual history in the Church of England: i) its deep roots in the early Christianity of the British Isles, planted firmly in the ancient, life-giving soil of Scripture, the Creeds and mission; ii) the recovery of these priorities in the 16th Century in order to proclaim a generous Gospel through its Prayer Book, Homilies, and Articles; iii) the spread of these formularies to North America and the eventual founding of the Episcopal Church; and finally iv) the recent Jerusalem Declaration which calls the Anglican Communion back to the foundational truths of the 16th Century and the emergence of the Anglican Church in North America to promote them. With wit and without rancor, Chuck gives just the facts, letting the power of the tradition draw his readers to the best insights of the past so that they may discover the way forward to their own better selves.

If that were not enough, however, this book also addresses specific key issues confronting American Christians in general. In the face of our country's pervasive cultural commitment to performance-based identity, Chuck points his readers to the Reformation's Gospel of Grace made possible by the performance of Christ for us on the cross. In the face of western society's relativism, pluralism and universalism, Chuck reminds his readers of the eternal truths of Scripture, the uniqueness of Christ, and the need for personally trusting him for salvation. In the face of rampant biblical skepticism, Chuck urges his readers to trust the One who inspired it and find its simple interpretation in both its immediate context and the Bible's overarching, unifying themes.

Finally, Chuck tackles questions that newcomers to the Church of England tradition might have about a prayer book as well as the sacraments of thanksgiving through Holy Communion and infant baptism. In all three areas, the Anglican Reformation chose the generous, balanced, middle way. In matters of liturgy, rather than keeping all the unscriptural additions of the medieval church or throwing out all written prayers entirely, if the ancient prayers still served to further the Gospel, the Church of England kept them. In baptism, rather than insisting that all recipients are automatically supernaturally changed as infants or that baptism was rightly reserved for a public testimony to being born-again when a person was old enough to make a decision for Jesus, Anglicans have historically believed that infant baptism conveyed a supernatural gift which recipients would still need to confirm personally when they came of age. In Holy Communion, rather than accepting the medieval doctrine of transubstantiation or merely a symbolic, memorial understanding, the architect of the first Anglican prayer books, Thomas Cranmer, taught the supernatural nature of Holy Communion, but that what was changed was not the bread and wine, but rather the recipient's heart – being crucified afresh with Christ by Christ.

A shrewd observer of the times, Chuck Collins knows that contemporary Americans can find wholeness only by going on a journey to those moments in history when the church was most fully alive. Softly and tenderly, he is calling deeply committed American Anglicans, as well as exploring newcomers, to come home to an authentically biblical, decidedly ancient and graciously generous way to be a disciple of Jesus Christ. Those wearied by the culture wars of today and longing for a compass to a better future will welcome the timeless truths of Chuck Collins' *Reformation Anglicanism: Generous – Biblical – Beautiful.*

Ashley Null
Humboldt-Universität zu Berlin
Palm Sunday 2014

Contents

Contents

Introduction

I am an Anglican because Anglicanism at its core is generously orthodox, is completely biblical, and liturgically beautiful.

The generosity in Anglicanism sets this church apart from other Protestant churches. For example, the Church of England determined early on that the Bible is God's unique and inspired revelation without saying that it speaks to every earthly thing. We affirm the reality of heaven and hell, explaining this by saying what the Bible says: that God has predestined Christians to life. We believe that grace is given in Holy Communion without saying that God is objectively, bodily present in the bread and wine. We determined that every aspect of our nature is affected by sin without saying that we are totally worthless. It is a compassionate and gracious view of doctrine and morals that sets this church apart, but generosity doesn't mean *anything goes*. The church that stands for nothing will fall for anything.

Anglicanism is defined and guided by the Bible. The 16th Century English reformers didn't see themselves as starting something new; they only wanted to return the church to the authority of the

Bible and to ancient consensual Christianity from which the Medieval Catholic Church had departed. The "Anglican formularies" that speak about what Anglicans believe all affirm that the Bible more than just "contains" or "speaks of" the Word of God, it is the Word of God written. It is the authority by which every other authority is judged.

But, more than anything else, what draws many to Anglicanism is beauty. The winsome beauty of God's character is deeply embedded in the dignity of Anglican worship and in its prayers. Theologian Richard Mouw tells the story of a friend of his who, in his late thirties, came to know the love of God. One Sunday, on his way to retrieve bagels and *The New York Times*, he passed by an Episcopal church [once the only expression of Anglicanism in America] in which the singing spilled over into the street. He went in because he was curious. He said that when they said the words "we have strayed from thy ways like lost sheep, and there is no health in us, have mercy upon us most merciful Father" he had a profound experience that he described as "coming home." When he finally got back to his apartment and his wife asked where he had been, he surprised himself and her when he said, "I think I just became a Christian!" Mouw went on to say that this couple started attending church the next week and were soon baptized.[i]

The chapters of *Reformation Anglicanism* were written over the thirty years I have been a priest, first in the Episcopal Church, and now in the Anglican Church in North America (ACNA). They were written to address issues about our history, the theological underpinnings of Anglicanism, and more practical matters of why we worship the way we do and what membership means. I wrote this specifically to instruct newcomers to Anglicanism about its distinctive characteristics and to help older members who have forgotten the strength and beauty of our heritage. I believe that I also speak for others when I say that I find that being Christian is the best way to be a human being, being Protestant is the best way for me to be Christian; and being Anglican is the best way for me to be Protestant.

This work is dedicated to all who are unafraid to examine their faith, especially to my children: Noel, Alison, Hope, and Andrew. This comes with my prayers for you, and anyone who might pick this up, even if it's the only thing to read in a laundromat, required reading for a new members class, or, punishment for acting up in youth group. I am grateful for the constant encouragement of my wife, Ellen, and the kind friendship and encouragement of the Rev. Dr. Bill Dickson, the Very Rev. Dr. Paul Zahl, the Rt. Rev. Dr. Fitzsimons Allison, Bud Davis, PhD, and a number of other friends who did the painful work of reading the first drafts and gave me valuable feedback. The Rev. Dr. Ashley Null, not only generously wrote the Forward for this book, but has been a true friend in every sense of that word. My thanks also, to Canon Ron Speers and Anglican House Publishers for their confidence in me, and for their strong support.

Years ago, I vowed to not pay attention to authors who have the annoying habit of making simple and obvious things complicated. My goal is just the opposite; I want to make the matters of the faith as reachable and understandable as they really are. To the extent that I have succeeded, to God be the glory!

Bible verses are from *The New Revised Standard Version*.

The Rev. Chuck Collins
Phoenix, Arizona
2014

Chapter 1

Henry VIII? Are You kidding?

Okay, so admit it: the popular idea that King Henry VIII started the Church of England, the mother church of all Anglican churches, is a little embarrassing. This is the same "Henry" who had a succession of six wives and had a few killed along the way! Sure, this 16th Century monarch was desperate for a male heir to the throne, and, sure, he wanted a divorce so that he could marry Anne Boleyn. But who wants the genesis of their denomination hinging on the runaway ambition of a desperate king of England? The facts of history save us the embarrassment. The Anglican Church did not start with Henry. In fact, we have a much earlier and nobler beginning.

The Church of England goes all the way back to Jesus Christ and the apostles. In the Creed Anglicans recite every Sunday we affirm our belief in the "catholic and apostolic" church. This means that we hold to Jesus and to the teaching of the apostles – as our founder and foundations. We are catholic (not "Roman Catholic") in that we subscribe to the teaching of the church that is true for all Christians at all times (i.e., "universal"). And we are "apostolic" because we believe that the Anglican Church has its origins and authority in the enduring truth of the apostolic teaching recorded in Holy Scripture. The doctrine of "Apostolic Succession" is the succession of teaching from one generation to the next, starting with the original apostles (2 Timothy 2:2), and this is symbolized in the laying on of hands from one bishop to the next.

No one knows for sure when Christianity first arrived in Great Britain. There's a far-fetched tradition that Joseph of Arimathaea (of biblical fame, Matthew 27:57) brought Christianity to the isles, along with the Holy Grail, the supposed cup of the Last Supper. It's more likely that traders or Roman soldiers first introduced Christianity in the 2nd and 3rd Centuries. Britain's first Christian martyr, St. Alban, was killed there in the 3rd Century. And three English bishops attended the Synod of Arles - France, A.D. 314, indicating that the church in England was somewhat organized by that date.

The most ancient form of Christianity in Britain is not Roman Catholicism, but "Celtic" Christianity. The Celts were not originally a Boston basketball team or a style of jewelry; rather, they were a loose association of Christians who subscribed to a simple, austere expression of Christianity. They were organized around monasteries with abbots instead of dioceses with bishops. It was an expression that highly valued nature, hermits, and monks. But because of the influence of such missionaries as Augustine, the Benedictine monk sent by the pope in A.D. 597, the church in Britain gradually turned towards Rome. At the Synod of Whitby (A.D. 664) the English church formally decided to follow the practices of the Latin Church over those of the Celts. But even with the new allegiance to Rome, British monarchs retained the right to approve all church appointments.

As the church moved into the Middle Ages, it evolved into something very different from the way it began. "Tradition" gradually began to assume a separate but equal status as an authority alongside the Bible. This opened the door for all kinds of extra-biblical and unbiblical practices and beliefs, including mandatory celibacy for clergy, purgatory (the idea that there is a state of temporary refinement or punishment after death), and the practice of praying to the saints instead of directly to God. Increasingly, salvation was considered something that could be earned by doing certain religious acts instead of God's gracious love and free gift. Holy Communion became an elaborate re-sacrifice on an altar in which bread and wine were thought to become the actual body and blood of Jesus Christ. What was originally meant to be "mystery" surrounding the Sunday services acquired a more "magical" quality (the term "hocus pocus" is derived from the Latin phrase for "This is my body"). The liturgy was recited in Latin and was barely understood by the clergy, much less by the average churchgoers. Added to the growing undercurrent of discontent was the terrible moral and educational decline of many of the clergy. It was not uncommon for priests to have mistresses, to use their ministry for financial gain, and to be absent from their churches for long periods of time.

John Wycliff (1320-1384) was "England's first true Protestant."[ii] By the time he arrived on the scene the pump was primed for the century long re-formation of the church that followed in his wake. Wycliff was the leading theologian and philosopher of Europe's most outstanding university, the University of Oxford. His aim, and the aim of all the English reformers, was to reinstate Holy Scripture as the primary authority for the church. This posed a clear and present challenge to the treasured traditions of the medieval Catholic Church. Adding fuel to the reforming fires were the writings of Martin Luther in Germany that were illegally finding their way into England. Especially affected by his inflammatory ideas was a group of English academics at Cambridge University (that included Cranmer and

Tyndale, mentioned later). The White Horse Tavern in Cambridge became the hangout for those interested in discussing the Bible and the German reformers. These religious stirrings, the invention of the moveable type printing press (1450), the translation of the Bible into English (1526), and the rise of humanism (encouraging the study of Hebrew and Greek) all paved the way for a major Reformation of the church in England.

At the same time that momentum for religious reformation was building, steam was also building on the political front. Henry VIII was looking for a political solution to dissolve his inconvenient marriage to Catherine of Aragon. He frantically wanted to father a male heir to the throne. In 1534, when the pope refused to act on his behalf, Henry took the advice of his new Archbishop of Canterbury, Thomas Cranmer, and declared that the Bishop of Rome had no authority over English bishops. By an act of Parliament, Henry was named the "supreme head" of the Church of England. After centuries of labor pains, political and theological, a distinct Church of England was born! Henry remained Roman Catholic in his beliefs and practices until he died, but by starting an independent branch of the Catholic Church he made a way for the religious and theological Reformation in England. He never embraced Protestantism as such, but he opened the door for the Reformation by legalizing the English Bible, abolishing monasticism in Britain, and having his son, the future King Edward VI, educated by Protestant mentors. It's significant that, on his deathbed, instead of asking for sacramental Last Rites, Henry reportedly came to a personal faith in Christ.[iii]

Anglicans are permanently linked to the Protestant principles of the English Reformation: the Bible as supreme authority (over tradition, reason, and experience), "Justification by Faith" alone through grace alone by Jesus alone (we can be "right" with God by receiving in faith what Jesus accomplished for us on the cross, not by being 'religious' or 'good'), and the "Priesthood of all Believers" (we don't need a priest, pope, or any other intermediary to relate to God personally).

Edward VI, Henry's son, ascended to the throne in 1547. Under Edward the Protestant rumblings of the previous 200 years finally coalesced, leaving "evangelical sympathizers in firm control."[iv] The boy King was nine years old when he was crowned and he ruled only six years before his untimely death. But enormous changes took place during those years. The Mass, formerly in Latin, was written in common English and called "Holy Communion." Communion tables replaced altars, and wine, previously reserved for clergy only, was distributed along with the bread to all communicants. Cranmer also led a team to produce 12 set sermons (Homilies) that, by royal order, were to be used throughout the realm. The Homilies explain the Reformational mindset of the Church of England.

When Edward was on his deathbed his protectors (he was merely a child of fifteen) had his will written to provide for the throne to succeed to the zealous Protestant, Lady Jane Grey. She held the throne for nine days before she was tried and convicted of high treason and received the penalty provided by the law: beheading. After Edward and Jane died the Church of England experienced a five-year reversion back to Catholicism under Queen Mary. She was called "Bloody Mary" because she ordered the killing of a number of prominent Protestant leaders. On her hit list was Archbishop Cranmer who was burned at the stake March 21, 1556. A month earlier, in a weak moment, Cranmer was persuaded to sign three recantations of his Protestant views. But, "of all the martyrs, strange to say, none at the last moment showed more physical courage than Cranmer did."ᵛ As the fire was burning around him he reportedly put his hand into the flames and said, "this unworthy right hand," referring to his previous recantation. He died bravely for the cause of the Protestant Reformation in England, having settled the Church of England into Protestantism by writing the first Prayer Books, and Anglicanism's confession, The Articles of Religion.

When Mary died Elizabeth became queen. She was the daughter of Henry VIII and fifth in the Tudor dynasty. She returned the church to Protestantism and brought a measured settlement to "Anglican"[vi] theology and worship that provided the room for important theologians, like John Jewel and Richard Hooker, to develop and define Anglicanism's generous orthodoxy. During her 45-year reign as queen (1558–1603), Elizabeth sought to balance the church's Scripture basis (i.e. Protestant) while not totally abandoning the beautiful parts of Catholicism. Unlike other Protestant churches born at the same time, a conscious decision was made to retain certain institutions (like bishops) and some ceremonial practices of the Catholic Church that did not conflict with the teaching of Holy Scripture.

While the English Reformation was theologically decisive in determining the future of Anglicanism, there were other influences as well. 16th Century Catholics, humanists and their offspring (Anglo-Catholics, rationalists, and Broad Church) have impacted Anglicanism at different times and in different ways making the "dialogue" alive and interesting. And the mantle of leadership has gone back and forth between these groups. But, while there is plenty of room for debate about secondary issues, there has been substantial agreement over the centuries about a fixed doctrinal core. The documents of the English Reformation, the key

Anglican theologians (including Cranmer, Hooker, Jewel and Andrews), and the Anglican formularies (including The Articles of Religion, the Homilies, and the Book of Common Prayer) all affirm a certain defining principle. Namely: the primacy, clarity and sufficiency of Holy Scripture is the final source of authority in the church and true for all people for all times.

This is a heritage to be proud of. Many Anglican laypersons and clergy have forever affected church and society. One literally gave his life to see the Bible translated into English – William Tyndale. Another wrote the first two versions of the Book of Common Prayer (1549 and 1552), enshrining the essentials of our Anglican heritage in the context of our worship – Thomas Cranmer. One wrote over 5,000 hymns, including "Hark! The Herald Angels Sing" – Charles Wesley. As a member of Parliament, another Anglican – William Wilberforce – led the movement that resulted in the abolition of slavery in England. It was an Anglican who wrote one of the most effective instruments to bring people to faith in Jesus Christ in modern times – *Mere Christianity* by C. S. Lewis. More presidents of the U.S. have been Anglican (i.e. Episcopalian) than of any other denomination, and courageous Anglicans around the world are known for upholding the biblical faith and as crusaders for the dignity of every human being.

CHUCK COLLINS

Chapter 2

Anglicans Weasel Into America

It's possible to visit an Anglican church today that transports you back to the Middle Ages: where incense is burned, elaborate clergy vestments are worn, and the Bible readings are chanted. And just down the street is another Anglican church where few or no formal vestments are worn, guitars have replaced the organ, and the minister is almost indistinguishable from an enthusiastic Baptist preacher. There are all kinds of Anglican churches: high and low, evangelistic and social action, traditional and charismatic. The differences are largely explained by how the Church of England was introduced to America.

Here's how it started. Although there were occasional Church of England services in America before 1600, the official birthday of Anglicanism in America, what later became the Episcopal Church, is generally agreed to be June 16, 1607. This is the day Captain John Smith and 104 others celebrated the Lord's Supper with their Church of England priest-chaplain, Robert Hunt, to commemorate their safe arrival to Jamestown, Virginia. Jamestown was the first permanent English colony in America, some thirteen years before the pilgrims landed in Plymouth. Anglicans were America's original forefathers! The expression of faith they brought with them was that of the 16th Century Protestant Reformation.[vii]

The word "Episcopal" is the English equivalent of the Greek word for "bishop." With this kind of emphasis it might be assumed that bishops played an important role in the early years of Anglicanism in America. Surprisingly, they were not in the picture at all! For almost two hundred years the Episcopal Church did not have a resident bishop to perform confirmations, ordain clergy, consecrate new churches, or form hierarchical diocesan structures. The Book of Common Prayer (i.e. a common theology) was the glue that kept the church together during its formative years. Many Puritans, some of them Anglicans, were perfectly happy with this arrangement because they believed that bishops from the Church of England would try to sway politics in England's favor in the colonies.

Between 1730 and 1745 the evangelical revival that began in England spilled over into America. "The Great Awakening," as it was called, was closely associated with Church of England evangelists. George Whitefield in America and his counterpart in England, John Wesley, both attracted huge crowds who were hungry for a personal relationship with the living Lord. Wesley started what was at first sarcastically called "Methodism." This renewal movement inside the Church of England taught the importance of personal faith for appropriating God's grace. Wesley remained an Anglican priest all his life, but soon after he died Methodist proponents left to form their own denomination. Regrettably, most members of the Church of England ignored Whitefield, Wesley, and the 18th Century revival, opposing the "religious enthusiasm" that often accompanied their ministry.

England's church in America at the time of the American Revolution was barely holding on by its fingernails. As the Revolutionary War heated up, many clergy returned to England because of their sworn allegiance to the crown. The Declaration of Independence (1776) signified many changes, among which was the inevitable break of the American Church of England into the first independent branch of Anglicanism.[viii] They changed the name in 1785 for obvious reasons from The Church of England to "The Protestant Episcopal Church in the United States of America." Even though it took some time to iron out the details for a new form of church governance, the main concern for the first Episcopalians "was to insure the continued existence of the faith, order, and worship of the Anglican Communion in the United States of America."[ix]

Two strong bishops dominated the early years of the Episcopal Church: Samuel Seabury and William White. These men represented two very different faith-expressions that competed against one another for the character of the Episcopal Church. Seabury was sent by Connecticut clergymen to England to seek consecration (ordination to be bishop). After an unsuccessful year of pleading with English authorities, he went to Scotland in 1784 where he was consecrated the first bishop of the Episcopal Church. As part of the agreement he made to be consecrated, Seabury agreed to introduce certain elements of the Scottish Prayer Book into the Episcopal Church. In the meantime, White was the rector of Christ Church in Philadelphia. At the urging of the Archbishop of Canterbury, White dismissed Seabury's consecration as invalid. The result was two rival Episcopal churches in the United States, one led by Seabury with an "irregular" consecration and the other by White who was not yet a bishop.[x] White was finally "properly" consecrated a bishop in England in 1787.

Seabury and White disagreed with one another about how to configure the new church. Seabury wanted a bishop-dominated structure like the English model while White argued for much greater priest and lay involvement based on the representative democratic model of the American political system. Seabury saw dioceses as the most important unit of ministry while White thought that bishops and dioceses exist only for the limited role of supporting local churches.[xi] After significant debate, Seabury conceded to White's proposals for an American Prayer Book, and both factions were brought together for the first General Convention of 1789. It was mostly White's ideas that shaped the Episcopal denominational structure, and, by way of its Prayer Book, its theology. He fought for and won the adoption of the Thirty-Nine Articles of Religion as the theological standard for the American Church. White also published a reading list that gave theological shape to several generations of priests ordained in the Episcopal Church.

White and Seabury also represented two different views of churchmanship. Generally speaking, White spoke from a foundation of Reformation or evangelical Anglicanism and Seabury from a high-church or Anglo-Catholic foundation.

Evangelicals believe that the key elements of Anglican theology were largely settled in the time period between Thomas Cranmer and Richard Hooker (1554-1600). Hooker, probably England's greatest theologian, wrote the famous Laws of

Ecclesiastical Polity against the Puritans who were professed followers of John Calvin. His main purpose in writing, however, was to show that the Church of England is planted on the teaching of the English Reformers who viewed the supremacy of Holy Scripture over tradition and reason, and founded on the doctrines of justification by faith alone by grace alone through Christ alone, and the Priesthood of all Believers. Anglican Puritans, on the other hand, trying to out-reform the Reformation, "were creating a novel theological synthesis that bore little resemblance to orthodox Christian thought."[xii]

Anglo-Catholics then and today view the Caroline Divines (from the mid 1600's) up through the Oxford Movement (Starting in 1833) as a settlement of previously developing Anglican theology.[xiii] They take their cue from pre-Reformation Catholic ideals. They view Scripture as a part of tradition because "the church wrote the Bible," and they adopted an interpretation of the Articles of Religion that largely ignored the force or place of the Reformation. They believe in Apostolic Succession as the succession of bishops traceable back to the original apostles over and above the idea of succession of teaching from one generation to the next (that is symbolized by the laying-on-of-hands to make someone a bishop). They taught "baptismal regeneration" – the idea that someone is automatically "born again" when they are baptized, whereas evangelicals spoke of the necessity of personal conversion. Anglo-Catholics were not at first ritualists, but before long Medieval Catholic elements in worship and ceremony made their way back into the church. After 1976 when the practice of ordaining women was forced on the church and the revision of the Prayer Book in 1979, different Anglo-Catholics pulled out of the Episcopal Church to start their own breakaway churches and denominations, sometimes called "the continuing churches." There are many Anglo-Catholics today who have locked arms with evangelicals in their common disgust for what the Episcopal Church has come to stand for, and they are working together in the Anglican Church in North America (ACNA).

Both evangelicals and Anglo-Catholics oppose the rationalism of the 16th Century humanists and especially the harsher side of the 18th Century Enlightenment. It can be a dangerous idea, the idea that everything, including the Bible, can be explained by human reason. From this came the critical study of Scripture ("biblical criticism"). Biblical criticism in its various forms started as something positive: to understand what the authors of Scripture were saying to the particular audiences for which they wrote. But human reason that doesn't take into account divine revelation (i.e. the Bible) is bound to fail in the end. In 1889 a collection of essays was published by a group of influential Oxford Anglican scholars *entitled Lux Mundi*: a series of Studies in the religion of the Incarnation. [xiv] This book sought to relate faith to "modern intellectual and moral problems," but its impact was to open Anglican's door to the new critical view of Holy Scripture. Anglicanism has never and is not today anti-intellectual. In fact it highly values a person's ability to intellectually question teaching and come to a personal faith. However, to interpret Scripture to fit an unrestrained confidence in science, social progress and a "sunnier picture of human nature"[xv] only opens the door to novel and unbiblical ideas. Some theologians' readiness to abandon the plain teaching of Holy Scripture in the name of "dynamic orthodoxy" or "progressivism" has toppled the pillars of what Episcopalians have always believed. Liberalism, once a moniker for open-mindedness and charitable consideration of other beliefs, has become a party label for a dogmatic and often-intolerant worldview governed by cultural trends and "what feels good."

Most Anglicans around the world consider themselves "evangelical" or Reformation Anglican. Of the more than 90 million Anglicans in the world, by far the vast majority of them (mostly in Africa and Asia) are evangelicals. Three notable times in Anglican history certain evangelical groups left to start their own churches: after John Wesley died many of his followers left the Church of England to form the Methodist Church; in 1873 a small group of evangelicals, led by the Assistant Bishop of Kentucky, George David Cummins, broke away to start the Reformed Episcopal Church; and in 2000 a group led by two newly consecrated bishops, Chuck Murphy and John Rogers, left the Episcopal Church to start the Anglican Mission in America (AMiA) as an extension of the Provinces of Rwanda and Southeast Asia. The courage of the original AMiA bishops, clergy and lay leaders gave courage for many others to leave the wavering Episcopal Church, most of them now under the umbrella of the Anglican Church in North America (ACNA). Orthodox Episcopalians have felt that they have no other choice but to continue to walk the path of historic Anglicanism wherever it leads. For some, this means staying in the Episcopal Church and fighting for its heart and soul; for others, it means walking into the refuge of historic Anglicanism that ACNA provides. (Both the Reformed Episcopal Church and the Rwanda outreach have become components parts of ACNA.)

Chapter 3

Believe It Or Not . . .

I eavesdropped on a conversation once in which a very nice lady said, "I love Anglicanism because you can believe anything and still be Anglican!" Do Anglicans believe anything? Or nothing? If you are looking for a church that will spoon-feed you their doctrine or tell you how to think, Anglicanism is not for you. This doesn't mean, however, that it stands for nothing. The church that stands for nothing will fall for anything! Within the "roominess" of this church is a rich heritage with clearly defined Anglican essentials.

First and foremost, the Anglican Church believes the Bible and believes in the Bible. We are the product of the 16th Century English Reformation whose primary purpose was to return the church to the Bible as its highest authority. But this doesn't mean that we are fundamentalists. Fundamentalists invented the terms "infallibility" and "inerrancy" to convey their commitment to the inspired authorship of the Bible, but in the process they tend to have overlooked its human aspects. Theological liberals, at the other extreme, tend to emphasize the human authorship while neglecting its divine origin and inspiration. They tend to discount the miracles and any connection there is between the sixty-six books of the Bible based on the single authorship of the Holy Spirit.

Anglicans have historically maintained a balance between these two views. We believe that real human beings wrote the Bible with evidence of their humanity found throughout. We also believe that God inspired them and blessed them in their writing to accurately communicate God's Word. This honoring of dual authorship (God and man) is what distinguishes Anglicanism from some of the other denominations. What an incredible miracle it is, for example, that the Apostle John's personality and his fisherman's understanding of the Greek language is found in the book of Revelation, and yet we still believe that God stands behind this book as its author and inspiration. It would have been a lesser miracle (and, no doubt, better grammar!) had God bypassed John's humanity – put him in some kind of God-trance – so that he could dictate every letter, word and sentence.

The primacy of Scripture means that Scripture is the norm of faith and morals, and the norm by which every other norm (creeds, tradition, confessions of faith, even "what feels good") is judged. All true Doctrine, Anglicans believe, is derived from the Bible... Article 6 of the Articles of Religion states: "whatever is not read therein, nor may be proved thereby, is not to be required of any man that it should be believed a an article of the Faith." (See also the ACNA Catechism: *To Be A Christian, An Anglican Catechism* [xvi]) Prayer Book revisions, for example, are allowed so long as "there be not any thing in it contrary to the Word of God" (Preface to 1789 Book of Common Prayer). We believe that God "caused" the Holy Scriptures to be written for our learning" (Collect for Proper 28). Every person ordained in the Anglican Church in North America declares in writing their allegiance to the Bible "to be the Word of God, and to contain all things necessary to salvation." (The Ordinal of ACNA) Anglicanism is also known as a "creedal church" insomuch as the creeds (Nicene Creed, the Creed of St. Athanasius, and that which is commonly called the Apostles' Creed) "may be proved by most certain warrants of Holy Scripture" (Article VIII, p. 869). And lastly, huge portions of Anglican liturgy in Prayer Books around the world are taken verbatim from the Bible.

Some American Anglicans like to talk about three sources of authority – Scripture, reason and tradition – as a "three-legged stool." The idea is that each leg is equally important and each is a necessary counterbalance for the other two. This tidy division of authority is valuable in one respect: it shows that Anglicans highly value reason and tradition. But, in fact, the idea of three equally weighted sources of authority is a modern invention that distorts what Anglicans have always believed. Theologian Richard Hooker, called "the inventor of Anglicanism," never used the analogy of a stool as some falsely claim. And he didn't speak of three equally weighted sources of authority. He did write about three *woven cords* (Scripture, reason, and tradition), but he consistently spoke of the primacy of Holy Scripture. [xvii] An analogy better fitting our Anglican heritage is recommended by the former dean of Nashotah House Seminary, Robert Munday: three ascending levels of a tower. He says, "Scripture is the foundation. Tradition rests on Scripture and is built upon it but cannot go where there is no foundation. Reason rests on Scripture and tradition and builds upon it but, again, cannot go where there is no supporting foundation." [xviii] The Bible preeminently serves Anglicans today as it always has: God's revelation and our primary source of authority. And reason and tradition (and experience) are to help us understand and apply God's Word to our lives.

It is also common parlance to say that Anglicans "believe what we pray" (*Lex orandi, lex credendi* – the law of praying is the law of belief). The idea is that the core of our beliefs are embedded in our prayers. But this is a recent idea that "has nothing to do with anything distinctly Anglican." [xix] In fact, we have always believed that prayers should reflect the truth of God's Word and not the other way around. Permission is given, for example, for periodically revising the Prayer Book, but with the proviso that the core doctrine (i.e., "essence of the faith") remains the same (1789 Preface to the Prayer Book).

It is commonly said that Anglicanism is not a "confessional church." This means that, unlike Lutherans who have the Augsburg Confession and Presbyterians with the Westminster Confession, we do not have a single defining statement of belief. But this doesn't tell the whole story. Even though we are not "confessional" in the same way, we do have the "Articles of Religion" (sometimes called "The Thirty-Nine Articles", pp. 867-876). These were written at the same time as the other great Protestant confessions with the same purpose in mind. The 1571 (and final) version of the Articles succinctly states their purpose: "For the avoiding of diversities of opinions and for the establishing of Consent touching true religion." It is clear that the original intent of the Articles was to establish the limits of Anglicanism's comprehensiveness at a time when Protestant extremists ("Anabaptists") and the Church of Rome were competing for a place in the English church. The Articles have enjoyed widespread and consistent support as Anglican's key doctrinal statement. At the General Convention of 1801, the fledgling American Episcopal Church, the parent of modern-day American Anglicanism, adopted the Articles as its theological standard.[xx]

While many in America have left the Episcopal Church to keep on the path of historic Anglicanism, the hope for Anglican's future in America is Anglican's past. In the summer of 2008 some 1,200 Anglican Bishops, clergy and laity from around the world gathered in Jerusalem at GAFCON (Global Anglican Futures Conference) to refocus the church's attention on the essentials that keep different kinds of Anglicans together. At this conference The Jerusalem Declaration was written, revised and fine-tuned by the best theological minds in the Anglican Communion. Among other things the Declaration affirms the uniqueness of Jesus Christ as humanity's only Savior, upholds the Bible as God's Word written, endorses the teaching of four Ecumenical Councils and the historic creeds, upholds the Thirty-nine Articles of Religion as containing the true doctrine of the Church and authoritative for Anglicans today, and commits to uphold Christian marriage between one man and one woman. The Jerusalem Declaration doesn't pretend to be a new "confession," but an affirmation of what Anglicans have always believed.

It is not exactly clear who first came up with this saying: "In essentials – unity; in non-essentials – liberty; and in all things – charity." But this is Anglicanism! It's a room big enough for lots of dialogue and different ideas, but its parameters are defined by certain essentials (i.e., biblical truth and the summaries of biblical truth in the creeds, the Prayer Book, and "Articles of Religion"). The Preface of the Prayer Book (from 1789) makes the important distinction between "doctrine" and "discipline." Discipline includes those matters that can and should change from time to time to make the church relevant to modern language and culture. This includes the words of our worship and prayers, and the moral and theological matters that the Bible doesn't address. Doctrine, on the other hand, is the "substance of the faith" that is true today as it has always been (Jude 3 "the faith once and for all delivered"). Doctrine includes the moral teachings on the many issues where the Bible is abundantly clear. Doctrine doesn't change over time because it is the core biblical teaching that is always true, always relevant, and always contemporary – "the grass withers, the flower fades; but the word of our God will stand forever" (Isaiah 40:8).

The nice lady I overheard was wrong. The most dangerous threat today to Anglican identity is the culture's infatuation with "tolerance. It sometimes seems more important to be polite than truthful, to celebrate our differences than to assert that we know something with confidence. Diversity – once only a description of the colorful variety that makes up our Church – has seemingly become for some the objective of our faith. A bishop I once heard said it is better to be loving than correct. This must be true, as far as it goes. But the good is the enemy of the best: the best is to be both loving and correct. In fact, something cannot be really "loving" unless it is based in "truth" ("Love rejoices in the truth" 1 Corinthians 13:6). To pursue unity at the expense of the truth does not lead to unity in the church, but unity of the church to the world. Jesus said that the Truth will make us free (John 8:32), not some hollow sentimentalism that embraces every teaching that comes down the road.[xxi] Hope for unity among Anglicans lies in our history that is founded on the enduring truth of God's revealed Word.

Chapter 4

Good News? Says Who?

So, WHAT do Anglicans believe? That's a big question that includes how we view God, our relationship to creation, and how we conduct our lives. There is obviously not enough space here to begin to address all these things, but we can identify the heart of the matter. It is called "the Gospel" or Good News. And the heart of the Gospel is not primarily the life of Christ or exhortations for Christians to "try harder" and "do more." In fact, the heart of the Christian message says nothing about what we do, but rather what God has done for us in his Son on the cross. As Presbyterian pastor, Tim Keller, is fond of saying, Jesus lived the life that we couldn't live and he died the death we deserve to die.

The Apostle Paul said, "May I never boast of anything except the cross of our Lord Jesus Christ." (Galatians 6:14). This is the thread, the master theme, which unites the whole Bible. The Old Testament foretells and the New Testament explains that Jesus "truly suffered, was crucified, dead, and buried, to reconcile his Father to us . . ." (Article II, p. 868). On a human level the cross is gruesome and bloody. But the Bible tells us that it is the crux around which all human history finds its meaning.

Jesus died on the cross to save us. But from what? And how did he do it? Something here must be said about: God, Human Nature, Jesus Christ, and Our Response.

GOD

There are two things that are essential to know about the God of the Bible: he is holy and he is loving. "Note then the kindness and severity of God..." (Romans 11:22).

God is *holy*. He is not "like us, only better." He is absolutely morally pure and free from sin and imperfection. God existed before time was invented and his kingdom has no end. His word is so powerful that by just speaking he brought everything into being from nothing. He never changes in His almighty power, wisdom, and justice that utterly surpasses our ability to comprehend. By his nature he detests sin and everything that is a contradiction to his holiness (Habakkuk 1:13). And since he is holy, God has made holiness the condition required for salvation. The Bible tells us that God is angry (wrathful) at sinful, self-centered humanity who set themselves against his plans and purposes. His is a holy anger, not a flying-off-the-handle kind. His anger is only appeased by righteousness: people, and ultimately all of creation, restored to a right relationship with God.

God is love. He acts lovingly, but it's more than that. So thoroughly is he loving that the Bible says that Jesus is love (1 John 4:16). And the best news of all is that his love is personal. The creator of all that exists knows the number of hairs on your head, and every sparrow that falls. He calls each of us by name! Even though we do not deserve it, he loves us. Even when we're at our worst, he never stops. No one, no matter how badly they have managed their lives, is beyond the reach of his love and forgiveness.[xxii] The word for this – highest of all loves – is "grace." The Bible tells us that God is like the father of completely rude and disrespectful sons (Luke 15). One son demanded his inheritance and then wasted it all on wild living. The father had every right to be furious, but the day he saw his son walking down the road toward home, he forgot to be angry because of his joy over his son's return. The older son was equally disrespectful and selfish, and undeserving of his father's love. But the father never stopped loving both boys with the same selfless love. God's love is his dominant attribute and the reason why he sent his only Son. God is always ready to welcome us home, to forgive our sins and extend to us the gift of a personal relationship. To crawl out of ourselves and into God's love is to enter into that special place of eternal security found only in the arms of our Heavenly Father.

HUMAN NATURE

Human beings are both "magnificent" and "miserable." This is our human condition. We are made in God's image AND we are miserable sinners.

According to the Bible, humans are the height of all creation, created in God's image to share his glory (Genesis 1:27). (Yet it has been calculated that the chemicals in a human body are worth less than $5 dollars at this writing!) But the Bible teaches that this arrangement of chemicals has immeasurable value to God. Unique in all of creation, humans are created to live in friendship with God. At the very least this means that we are more than flesh and bones; we have a living soul and God's life is breathed into us. Adam and Eve, the first humans, are pictured as strolling in the garden and chatting with God as friends. To be created in his image means that we have the God-given capacity (but not the guarantee) to relate to God as children to a father. Our highest purpose on earth is to enjoy this relationship. But just as the Bible teaches that we are created in God's image, it also teaches that creation was quickly followed by the entry of pride and self-righteousness into human hearts (Genesus 3). When

Adam and Eve disobeyed God (i.e., "the Fall"), evil effects came to all creation. Because of our connection to our most distant disobedient relatives, we are by nature selfish, prideful, and resistant to anyone telling us what to do – including God. Our sinful bent is called "original sin." The popular view that we are just a little dirty in need of a little cleaning up is not the biblical view. St. Paul put is this way, "All have sinned and fall short of the glory of God," and "There is no one who is righteous, not even one" (Romans 3:9,23). In another place he writes, "You were dead in your trespasses and sins . . ."(Ephesians 2:1). [xxiii] Even though we have the capacity to be friends with God (i.e., created in his image), we are by nature heading in another direction because of our sinful orientation. In even our best human efforts to be good and religious, because we are sinners we are unable to reach up to God and meet the requirement for righteousness. Something drastic, something earthshaking, had to happen from outside of us in order for us to have hope to heal our relationship with God.

JESUS CHRIST

The Bible makes perfectly good sense in the light of its central theme: Jesus Christ, the Savior of the world. Only someone who is fully God and fully man could heal the breach caused by human sin.

The baby born in Bethlehem's barn 2,000 years ago was a real human being. It is mind-boggling to think that Jesus dirtied his diapers and wailed when he was hungry like every baby. He had human emotions – love, sorrow, anger, and compassion. The Bible tells us that he experienced hunger, thirst and, sometimes, sheer exhaustion. Even though he experienced prophetic insights and supernatural knowledge not experienced by everyone, he also showed his full humanity by asking real questions, felt a need to pray regularly in order to stay close to his heavenly Father, and was tempted in every way that we are. It was real blood that came from his pain-racked body on the cross. Yet, in the fullness of his humanity, the Scriptures tell us (amazingly!) that he never sinned.

It's incredible to think that the baby that needed the touch and comfort of his mother was his mother's Maker and Savior! Jesus was flesh-and-bones man, but also God. "Immanuel" means "God is with us." He existed before he took on human form from the beginning, before there was time or anything created. One day, in the course of human history, he stepped out of his home in heaven to become one of us. "The Word became flesh and lived among us" (John 1:14). He did this to show that he would do anything and everything to reach us and save us. He temporarily and voluntarily put aside his divine prerogatives (God is everywhere, but the man-God Jesus confined himself to one locality at a time; God knows everything, but Jesus asked "Who touched me?" (Mark 5:38); God has all power even to bring into existence everything from nothing, but Jesus could do just a few healings in his hometown "because of their unbelief" (Matthew 13:58). He was fully man, but never for a minute did he give up also being God.

How then could the holy love of God come to terms with the unholy sinfulness of men and women? The answer – in fact the only answer – is the cross.[xxiv] The only way God could simultaneously express his holiness and love was by becoming the substitute that would give us a righteous standing before God. The only substitute worthy enough for our salvation was the God-man, the Lamb of God that takes away the sin of the world (John 1: 29, 36). Jesus was born to die. That's why almost half of each of the Gospels is devoted to the last few days of his life, focusing on the crucifixion. Instead of imposing on us the punishment we deserved, God in Christ endured it for us. Jesus took on himself the full weight of God's holy wrath so that we could be restored to a right relationship with God. He bridged the gap caused by our sin. So completely was he our substitute on the cross, according to the Bible he actually "became sin" (literally "became the sin-bearer") so that "in him we might become the righteousness of God" (2 Corinthians 5:21). Paul put it this way, "Christ redeemed us from the curse of the law by becoming a curse for us" (Galatians 3:13). In Peter's first letter he wrote: "He himself bore our sins in his body on the cross . . ." (1 Peter 2:24). And the writer of Hebrews said Christ was "offered once to bear the sins of many" (Hebrews 9:28).

The Bible teaches us that Jesus' death and resurrection had cosmic dimensions. Not only did he pay the full price for our salvation, but he once and for all won victory over evil and the powers of the devil. "The Son of God was revealed for this purpose, to destroy the works of the devil" (1 John 3:8). In another place John wrote that the ruler of this world has been condemned" (John 16:11). And the writer of Hebrews added, "that through [Christ's] death he might destroy the one who has the power of death, that is, the devil" (Hebrews 2:14).

Such is his grace! We can be forgiven of our sins because Jesus died for us. We can leave our self-centeredness and begin a new life centered on Jesus Christ because, through his death and resurrection, he has opened the way.

SO WHAT?

From our human perspective we are converted (or, go from spiritual death and rise to everlasting life) when we accept God's gift of salvation. It is free to us, but it cost him the life of his only Son. The Bible teaches that we are saved because we are elected and predestined to be saved. So from when we begin to be curious about the Truth – to the people he put in our lives to tell us about the Truth and pray for us – to receiving the gift of faith to accept the truth – it is God's doing absolutely and completely. Steve Brown captures the dynamic between God and humans when he wrote: "You take the first step, God will take the second step, and by the time you get to the third step, you will know that it was God who took the first step."[xxv]

Religion, if it is understood as good morals and becoming a better "me," never saved anyone. Religion like that just reinforces our natural self-righteousness, self-sufficiency, and self-confidence that is the exact opposite of a life centered in Jesus Christ. "The death of Christ renders anachronistic all attempts to satisfy the law by means of performance or achievement. Christ is the end of merit." [xxvi] Christianity, at its heart, is not a religion but a *relationship*. We could be the beneficiaries of a million dollars and still live in poverty because we have not cashed the check. Such is the condition of everyone who has not called on the name of the Lord, or who trusts in their baptism and not in personal conversion for their salvation, or believes more in what they "do" rather than what God has done for them. Paul in Romans writes, "If you confess with your lips that Jesus is Lord and believe in your heart that God raised him from the dead, you will be saved" (Romans 10:9). Then he went on to make what was simple even simpler: "Everyone who calls on the name of the Lord shall be saved" (v. 13). John says it this way: "To all who receive him, who believe in his name, he gave the power to become children of God" (John 1:12).

We love him only because he first loved us (1 John 4:19). As poet Francis Thompson said, God is the hound of heaven who pursues us until we find him. Because of our fallen nature we do not have it within ourselves to turn to God in faith (Article X). Therefore, if we are in a faithful, loving relationship with him it is because he has elected us and predestined us for such a relationship (Article XVII). The Bible explains this restored relationship in various ways: being born again (John 3), being accounted righteous before God (Romans 4), being saved (Romans 10), being justified by faith (Romans 5). Paul, writing to the Ephesians, put it this way: "For by grace you have been saved through faith. And this is not your own doing; it is the gift of God, not a result of works, so that no one may boast" (Ephesians 2:8).

It's not what we do for God that counts for salvation, but what he has done for us. Have you confessed your need of Him? Asked him to forgive your sins? Prayed for him to fill your life with his holy and life-giving Spirit? If you haven't and would like to – if you feel that God has brought you to this critical point in your life and he is pushing on you to enter into relationship with him – you can do it right now. In your heart of hearts you can pray a prayer like this:

> Jesus, I see that the emptiness I feel is because I was made to be in relationship with you, but I have sinned and lived selfishly. It is a wonder that you never gave up on me. Thank you for offering me a new beginning: a way back to my Creator, Redeemer and Savior. Please forgive my sins. Please fill me with your holy and life-giving Spirit. Please receive me as a wayward child to my waiting, loving Father, as a sinner to my Savior. I ask this, not because I deserve it because I don't, but because you love me and lived the perfect life I cannot live in order to fulfill the law on my behalf, and you died on the cross as my substitute so that I can have eternal life. With the faith you give me, I now accept the gift of new life in the name of the Trinity: Father, Son and Holy Spirit. AMEN.

Like some of you, I grew up in the Episcopal Church and I have lots of good memories about it. But I don't remember a time as a child or as a young person hearing the Gospel explained. And I can't remember a time in Sunday school or in a church service when I was invited to accept God's free gift of salvation. It was only later that I accepted Jesus as my Lord and Savior, responding to his love. And it was much later that I realized, to my utter surprise, that this gospel message is something so deeply

"Anglican" that we hear it regularly in our Sunday worship service, that is, about God, and Human Nature, and Jesus Christ

> "Holy and gracious Father: In your infinite love you made us for yourself; and, when we had fallen into sin and become subject to evil and death, you, in your mercy, sent Jesus Christ, your only and eternal Son, to share our human nature, to live and die as one of us, to reconcile us to you, the God and Father of all." (p.362).

Chapter 5

Messiah of the Month Club

The setting was a college campus in Winter Park, Florida and the speaker was fiery and adamant. "Who would be so ignorant as to believe that Jesus is the only way to God?" John Spong, now the retired Episcopal bishop of the Diocese of Newark, went on to say, "Such a judgment would obviously exclude millions of respectable and moral Jews, Hindus, and Muslims – the majority of the human race! This exclusivity would be totally out of character with a loving God." Then he drove the point home with the ever-popular "All roads lead to God and we must respect one another." As you might imagine, the college audience indicated their approval with enthusiastic applause.

The idea that all religions more or less say the same thing or represent different paths to the same God is widely accepted today. "Pluralism," as it is called, says that it doesn't matter what you believe as long as you are sincere. This appeals to our Anglican sensitivities that value politeness very highly. And the reluctance to say that we know anything with certainty, what one theologian calls "a fashionable preference for doubt,"[xxvii]excuses us from responsibility to objective truth and leaves us with only the subjective kind that says, 'Christianity is true for me.'

Is that right? Is Jesus one of many ways? Or did God reveal himself fully and decisively in Jesus Christ alone? What do Anglicans believe?

To begin with, everyone knows that tolerance as a virtue has obvious limits. No one would tolerate a dog that bites everyone it meets, and an abused wife who tolerates her husband's beatings is to be pitied, not commended. It is also obvious that different religions are really different. Who would argue that Christianity and animism and Satanism are equally valid responses to God? Christianity and Islam, two of the world's great religions, are also clearly different. To take just one example: the New Testament hinges on the fact that Jesus died on the cross, while the Qur'an, Islam's bible, is equally emphatic that he did not. These are absolutely foundational teachings of both faiths and both can't be true. Furthermore, how are all religions basically the same if their goals are patently different? Christians hope for resurrection to everlasting life; Hindus envision reincarnation; and Rastafarians look forward to paradise where blacks are served by menial whites. To ignore the glaring differences might seem broad-minded, but in fact it is the worst kind of narrow-mindedness. To assert that all religions are essentially the same is a slap in the face to millions of people around the world who see the distinctives of their religion as critical. Christians should humbly and lovingly respect people of all faiths and work with them where we can for the goals that we share. But there's a big difference between respecting other religions and regarding all of them as equally valid roads leading to a common salvation.

The God of the Bible is not squeamish about distinctions even if we are. Scripture teaches unequivocally that followers of other religions are being led by deceptive spirits who oppose the God who created us and loves us. For example, the first two of the Ten Commandments – have no other gods, make no idols – show that God regards it a serious offense to become involved in other religions. "I will bring judgment on all the gods of Egypt," he said, and "Do not go after other gods" (Exodus12:12; Jeremiah 35:15). In addition, the Bible is unembarrassed to make extraordinary claims about the uniqueness of Jesus and to assert his superiority over other gods. This is what those who met him said about him "Never has anyone spoken like this!" (John 7:46), "Lord, to whom shall we go? You have the words of eternal life" (John 6:68), "Go away from me, Lord, for I am a sinful man!" (Luke 5:8), "Who then is this, that even the wind and sea obey him?" (Mark 4:41), "You are the Messiah, the Son of the living God" (Matthew 16:16), and "My Lord and my God!" (John 20:28).[xxviii]

Not only does the Bible teach that Jesus is "the only begotten Son of God" (words of the Nicene Creed), it also teaches that he is the only way to salvation. On the day of Pentecost Peter preached that "there is salvation in no one else, for there is no other name under heaven given among mortals by which we must be saved" (Acts 4:12). Jesus himself said, "I am the way, and the truth, and the life. No one comes to the Father except through me" (John 14:6). And Paul said, "there is one God; there is also one mediator between God and humankind, Christ Jesus . . . who gave himself as ransom for all" (1 Tim. 2:5). Anglican theologian Michael Green wrote, "Our forefathers in the faith died for their witness to the uniqueness and supremacy of Jesus as Lord and Savior. It is not for us to betray them and him in our generation."

"Grace" is what distinguishes Christianity from all other religions. Grace is best understood alongside the more widely accepted philosophy of "karma" – the belief that we get what we deserve. Grace says precisely the opposite: we get what we don't deserve. The unmerited and undeserved love of God for sinners makes Christianity unique from all other religions. Are there other saviors who love humans with perfect constancy even when they are behaving badly? Is there another god who invested himself so fully in humankind that he became one of us to rescue us? Is there another savior who washed his disciples' feet or willingly submitted to death on a cross? Is there another salvation that is based on the certainty of God's goodness and perfection rather than ours? Only Christianity teaches that God in Christ saved the world for those who haven't earned it, can't do enough to earn it, and would never have a hope for salvation if God hadn't stepped in to remedy the situation. "See what love the father has given us that we should be called the children of God!"(1John 3:15). No other religion teaches that we are saved because God loves us beyond our wildest imaginations.

But some take the idea of "grace" and bend it to say that everyone will be saved and go to heaven. They can't bring themselves to believe that God's love would ever exclude anyone. This is called "universalism." But this is not the teaching of Christianity. The Bible distinguishes between common grace and saving grace. Everyone, Christian or not, at some level knows there is a God, and that everything in creation that is beautiful, just and honorable points in some way to its Creator – common grace (Romans 1:20; 8:22). But Scripture also teaches that those who are Christian, who, by faith, have been adopted as God's children through the merits and mediation of Jesus Christ, have this relationship because of the saving grace of God. We love God because he first loved us (Romans 3:10; 1 John 4:19), and it is by grace that we are saved, totally independent of any good work we might or might not do (Ephesians 2:8). Every Christian is Christian because they are saved by grace alone, through faith alone, by Christ alone.

As Oxford theologian Alister McGrath, said, "it is a small step from the optimistic affirmation that 'all will be saved' to the authoritarian pronouncement that 'all must be saved' – whether they like it or not."[xxix] The same Bible that teaches us about heaven also teaches that God will send to hell those who refuse his saving grace. C. S. Lewis said "there are only two kinds of people in the end: those who say to God, 'Thy will be done,' and those to whom God says, in the end, 'Thy will be done.' All that are in Hell, chose it."[xxx] Universalism is an understanding based on wishful thinking, not on the Word of God.

The Bible's exclusive claim that God has come to earth in Jesus Christ causes serious heartburn in some circles. But there are only a few options for Christians: we can dismiss the Bible entirely as a dusty old book without relevance for today; or we can selectively apply its meaning to say that it is simply mistaken and culturally bound on this or that subject; or we can accept it as God's true plan and purpose that should shape what we believe. If we take the Bible seriously, there's no getting around what it says about Jesus.

Anglicans, then, are both inclusive and exclusive. God gives his common grace to all; he gives his saving grace to those who have eternal life according to God's own choosing (see Article XVII). We believe that Jesus is humanity's only Savior from sin, judgment and hell. In all of human history, only Jesus was both fully God and fully man. There is only one way to salvation: "For Scripture doth set out unto us only the Name of Jesus Christ, whereby men must be saved" (Article XVIII).[xxxi]

Even though we believe that Jesus is the only way to God, this doesn't mean that we are ready to condemn to hell those who have not heard the gospel. Only God will finally determine who's in and who's out. Only God is judge, and I'm sure that there will be surprises when we get to heaven. Once when Jesus was asked if many would be saved, he basically said, "That's up to me; just make sure you're in!" (My loose interpretation of Luke 13:23)

How then are we to think about our family members and friends who don't personally know Jesus Christ as their Lord? What if your brother follows another religion or your boss is an atheist?

Understandably, the last thing we want is to be judgmental or condemning. Christian claims about the exclusive nature of salvation are hard for many people, especially in our western culture where there are few values more important than tolerance and diversity. But if it's true that the God who created the universe, and humans to be in relationship with him, has provided a way for us to be reconciled with our creator through his Son Jesus Christ – and, if it is true that on this matter very literally hinges the question of where someone will spend eternity – then, Christians would be the most selfish people in the world to not enthusiastically share the most hopeful message they have ever heard. It's not a superior attitude, but a loving and humble heart that drives Christian evangelism because we are all too aware that we are "unworthy so much as to gather the crumbs from thy table" (Prayer of Humble Access, BCP p. 337). It's not that Christians are better than anyone else; just the opposite. You don't get into hell by being bad; you get into heaven by being bad and accepting forgiveness. [xxxii] This makes us both humble and grateful for God who loves us anyway. We serve the world as one beggar telling other beggars where we found bread. [xxxiii]

Are all religions one? No, clearly not! The fiery Episcopal bishop, in his zeal for tolerance, denies the hopeful truth about Jesus Christ. He is mistaken about one of the central teachings of Christianity and he is guilty of deceiving others. The centrality and uniqueness of Jesus Christ, called the "scandal of particularity,"[xxxiv] is anything but scandalous to those who are spiritually hungry, those who are looking for God's own remedy for the hunger that they feel.

Chapter 6

Does Anyone Care About the Trinity Anymore?

It is common to hear that the Holy Trinity is an idea too deep for normal Christians to understand. After all, the math doesn't add up: how can three be one – one God in trinity of Persons? The doctrine of the Trinity is often dismissed as a "mystery" that was interesting for a few early church fathers, but not today. This is nonsense, of course.

The Trinity is a central teaching about God in the Bible. Although the *word* "trinity" is nowhere mentioned in Holy Scripture, the *doctrine* itself is plainly and gloriously taught there. And although God indeed *is* bigger than our ability to fully comprehend him (otherwise he wouldn't be God), we can certainly know him as he reveals himself in Holy Scripture.

The doctrine of the Trinity can be stated very simply. St. Augustine, the sinner who dramatically turned world-class theologian (345-430), summed it up in seven simple statements:

1. The Father is God
2. The Son is God
3. The Holy Spirit is God

(and because the three are not just different names for the same thing . . .)

4. The Father is not the Son
5. The Son is not the Holy Spirit
6. The Holy Spirit is not the Father

(and because there are not three Gods . . .)

7. There is only one God

The Trinity is suggested in the plural titles used for God at critical places in the Bible (e.g. "Let *us* make man in our image" Genesis 3:22). The Bible attributes the creation to the Father (Psalm 102), to the Son (Colossians 1), and to the Holy Spirit (Genesis 1:2). Each of the persons of the Trinity is referred to as God; each is shown to be equal to the other two; and the threefoldness is affirmed in Jesus' baptism (Matthew 3) and in The Great Commission (Matthew 28).

The doctrine of the Trinity was exposed in Scripture when orthodox Christianity butted heads with heretics. For example Arius said that Jesus was not eternal – tantamount to saying that Jesus was not

God. Sebellius taught that the one God reveals himself in three ways – thus there are not three Persons of the Trinity, i.e., just three ways that humans experience God. And the Gnostics treated the Son (the Logos) as emanating from the Father and therefore not coexistent with the Father. But Anglicans hold to the orthodox Christian position that "there is but one living and true God . . . and in the unity of this Godhead there be three Persons, of one substance, power and eternity; the Father, the Son, and the Holy Ghost." (Article I).

Doctrine matters. The revealed truth of Scripture matters. If it doesn't matter here, then it doesn't matter when we search for meaning in Jesus' crucifixion, or for what God says about the sanctity of life or his will for the gift of sex and marriage. When we don't have the anchor of doctrine we can easily drift into "experience" as a constantly-moving substitute anchor that permits us to say just about anything about anything. The doctrine of the Trinity matters because God matters – because God's revealed truth matters – because God has shown us what he wants us to know about who he is and what he is like.

Just a few minutes before Jesus ascended into heaven he delivered his parting words to his disciples: The Great Commission (Matthew 28). Among other things he told them to baptize all new disciples in the name of the Father, and of the Son, and of the Holy Spirit. But what did Jesus mean when he said *baptize* them in the *name* of 'the Trinity?'" The idea of pouring water over bald and hairy heads three times to usher them into the New Covenant Community (as the rite of circumcision did in the Old Covenant Community) is certainly part of the meaning of baptism. When Jesus said *baptize* he meant this and also something much deeper and more profound.

Baptism is a borrowed term from the secular world that literally means: "to immerse or saturate," like someone might thrust a cloth into a vat of dye so that every fiber is saturated. And names were so very much more meaningful in biblical times than they are today because then they were chosen, or changed, to express the true nature of a person (or the hope of parents that their children would live into their names). Therefore, when Jesus asked the disciples to baptize new believers in the name of the Father, Son and Holy Spirit, he was asking that they be saturated by God himself, his Name, his character, his nature. Jesus' focus in The Great Commission is not so much on a liturgical rite of baptism, as important as it is, but that new believers will be thoroughly in God and God thoroughly in them – that every fiber of their being will be affected.

Now that's good news!

"Almighty God, you have revealed to your Church your eternal Being of glorious majesty and perfect love as one God in Trinity of Persons: Give us grace to continue steadfast in the confession of this faith, and constant in our worship of you, Father, Son, and Holy Spirit; for you live and reign, one God, now and for ever. Amen." (Prayer Of the Holy Trinity, BCP p.251).

Chapter 7

Sin – Not Promiscuous Genes

Several years ago a bishop in Scotland announced that some people have a "gene" that predisposes them to commit adultery, in other words, a promiscuous gene. When the word hit the press "Alleluias" could be heard all the way around the world! This revelation of the Primate [i.e., the head bishop] of the Episcopal Church in Scotland, Richard Holloway, was welcome news for every man looking for a way to explain the lipstick stains on his shirt collar! Is Bishop Holloway right? Can we not help ourselves? There is certainly something or other that strongly predisposes us to have multiple sex partners, but just what is it? What Bishop Holloway blames on biology is actually caused by a universal human predicament, a moral bent strongly towards tickling our fancy – what theologians call "original sin." Face it, we love sin.

Even if genes have something to do with our moral makeup (a proposition still to be determined), this doesn't mean that we are helpless victims. There is a higher authority than, "I felt the urge!" Urges, impulses, and giddy feelings are notoriously unreliable sources for determining God's will. Just because a person feels the urge to steal, get drunk, or slap their spouse around doesn't make it right any more than the urge to commit adultery makes that right. The temptations may be strong, even very strong, but we always have a choice to live for the promises we made in our wedding vows. What differentiates animals from human beings, after all, is that animals (and apparently a few priests and bishops!) are ruled by their appetites and do not yield to a higher standard. The Apostle Paul assures us that "God is faithful, and he will not let you be tested beyond your strength, but with the testing he will also provide the way out so that you may be able to endure it" (1 Corinthians 10:13).

Should we revise our ethical standards to accommodate the victims of promiscuous genes? (Satirist Garrison Kiellor invented a fellow named Bob, the founder of Bobism – "The religion that changes to meet your needs!") Is there an "Anglican" way of addressing ethical questions? What measure do we use to determine right from wrong?

First, if you want a list of acceptable and unacceptable behaviors you will be disappointed in Anglicanism. Occasionally some church convention will make unbinding and sometimes bizarre moral pronouncements, but, other than the Bible, we don't have an official code for moral conduct. Our goal is less to tell Anglicans how to act, than to encourage them to have Christian (i.e., biblical) minds and world-views, and instruct them to act accordingly. Unlike some denominations, we give strong deference to an individuals' ability to make personal moral choices based on the sources of authority available to them. This means that the same Anglican methodology that guides the study of theology also guides moral theology. Namely, the Bible is the primary authority, and reason and tradition are helpful in understanding and applying God's Word to our lives. For someone to reach a determination about the morality of war or abortion or premarital sex, to be "Anglican," it will have the support of Scripture, supported by reason, and tradition.

Using "adultery" as an example, is there a consistent and clear teaching about this in the Bible? Yes, the Bible plainly says that marriage is a life-long monogamous union of a man and woman (Genesis 2:24; Matthew 19:4-6). And even though early civilizations, yes, including the Israelites, practiced polygamy, the Bible consistently moves toward one-man-one-woman relationships as God's highest plan. It prohibits all sexual relations outside of marriage (e.g., Exodus 20:14, Matthew 5:27-28), and it uniformly calls adulterous relationships *sinful* (e.g.,

John 8:3). There is no wavering in the biblical teaching about this. Nowhere is adultery shown in a positive light, and everywhere it is condemned as wrong. The church throughout history has upheld this interpretation (tradition), and the social sciences confirm that adultery is destructive to families and other social institutions (reason).

Can a bishop then, even the Primate of the Scottish Episcopal Church, approve of such a practice? Not unless he is willing to leave the parameters of what the Anglican Communion teaches. And any bishop who finds themself outside the teaching of the church should resign or be booted out by their fellow bishops.

The same methodology of considering the Bible, reason, and tradition can be used to evaluate every moral issue. But what about the Bible? Who hasn't heard, "the Bible doesn't condemn homosexuality (or whatever controversial issue), it's just how you interpret it." This suggests that the Bible is a wax nose that can be shaped to fit our preconceived ideas. So why bother? If the Bible is the primary authority for Anglicans, how can someone read and interpret it with confidence for discerning God's will? Well, over Christian history a consensus of helpful principles has emerged.

FIRST, THE PRINCIPLE OF *INSPIRATION*

Anglicans affirm the Bible is God's inspired Word – he "caused the Holy Scriptures to be written for our learning" (Collect for Proper 28, p.184). And the best interpreter of any book is its author. When we read the Bible we consider that it is "from God" and we seek to live in line with its teaching. We ask the Holy Spirit's help so that we can understand it. The Holy Spirit enlightens those who are spiritually alive: "Those who are unspiritual do not receive the gifts of God's Spirit, for they are foolishness to them, and they are unable to understand them because they are spiritually discerned" (1Corinthians 2:14). Instead, he enlightens the humble: ". . . You have hidden these from the wise and intelligent and have revealed them to infants" (Matthew 11:25). And lastly, the Holy Spirit enlightens those who are willing to obey: "Anyone who resolves to do the will of God will know whether the teaching is from God or whether I am speaking on my own" (John 7:17). As we approach the Bible we want to have the same attitude as the Psalmist: "Open my eyes so that I can see what you show me of your miracle-wonders. I'm a stranger to these parts; give me your clear directions" (Psalm 119:18 *The Message*, Eugene Peterson).

SECOND, THE PRINCIPLE OF *SIMPLICITY*

This is the practice of looking for the natural or plain meaning of the text. The Bible is a revelation not an obscuration, and God's purpose is to lead us to truth not boggle our minds. Therefore, we will interpret a passage considering its literary type: history as history, poetry as poetry, and allegory as allegory. Lots of mistakes are made when we assume one literary type for the whole Bible (e.g., forcing a history, scientific view on Genesis 1-11; or assuming the New Testament is poetry/myth with a few hard-to-find glimpses of the real historic Jesus thrown in). The natural meaning is not necessarily the literal meaning – Jesus is not literally sitting on God's right hand, and he is not a literal wooden door of a sheepfold. And parables are stories of common everyday scenes that are meant to tell us something about the Kingdom of God. They are meant to shake us into realizing some great truth about God, not to be dissected and significance assigned to every little detail. This is the impact the parables would have had for those who first heard them. The principle of simplicity requires that we interpret Scripture based on the most natural meaning of a text.

THIRD, THE PRINCIPLE OF *CONTEXT*

As much as we can know from the surrounding verses and the overall message of a particular book, what was the author's original meaning? What did the original hearers hear and understand? Who wrote it? To whom? For what reasons? Resources, such as Bible commentaries and dictionaries can be helpful. Sometimes a passage that seems culturally bound and irrelevant is applicable today in terms of the principle behind it. For example, Paul teaches in 1 Corinthians that women are to keep their heads covered (11:5). In the 1st Century, covering heads was a symbol of submission to authority. Even though women are obviously not expected to wear hats today, the principle related to authority still applies. Only when we have ascertained as best we can what the meaning of the passage was to the original hearers can we accurately begin to apply it to our lives today. The principle of context precludes us from imposing our modern prejudices upon the ancient text.

FOURTH, ANOTHER PRINCIPLE OF BIBLE INTERPRETATION IS THE PRINCIPLE OF *UNITY AND HARMONEY*

Since God stands behind the Bible as its author and inspiration we interpret it as a whole rather than as sixty-six separate books without any real connection to one another. This means first that both testaments are the Word of God and complement each other, "for both in the Old and New Testament everlasting life is offered to Mankind by Christ" (Article VII). Additionally, it means that we will not "expound one place of Scripture, that it be repugnant to another" (Article XX). A teaching or doctrine cannot be considered biblical unless it sums up and includes all that the Bible says about it. Therefore, it is unhelpful to pull out isolated verses to support our pre-formed conclusions if the verses do not account for the overall teaching. This is called "proof-texting."

We also believe that God progressively revealed his Word over time so that if there is tension between the older and the newer portions of Scripture, the older will give way to the newer. A good example of this is the way the Bible addresses the status of women. In older biblical cultures women were considered property and non-persons, but they were given increasing dignity and honor from ancient Israel up to the New Testament. Jesus, especially as he is pictured in Luke's gospel, was the champion of "women's rights" in his day. And Paul – clearly challenging the male-dominated culture of the 1st Century – put men and women on the same footing for salvation (e.g., Galatians 3:28). This was counter-cultural and quite revolutionary! Many theologians feel justified in supporting women in ministry (and opposing the practice of slavery) based on the progression they see in the Bible. The principle of unity and harmony requires us to keep an eye on the overall teaching of Holy Scripture. And the final principle is:

FIFTH AND LASTLY, THE *CATHOLIC PRINCIPLE*

An interpretation of a particular passage of Scripture can be tested for accuracy by whether or not it is supported by the theological consensus of historic Christianity. This doesn't elevate tradition to the same place as the Bible, but it gives tradition the job of confirming an accurate interpretation. Vincent of Lerins, a 5th Century monk, described this as "that faith which has been believed everywhere, always, by all," and theologian Thomas Oden calls this "the ancient consensual tradition of Spirit-guided discernment of scripture."[xxxv]

The English Reformers, our Anglican forefathers, read deeply not only the Bible but also the writings of the early church fathers. They believed that the same Holy Spirit who inspired the writers of Scripture protected the Word of God over time. This doesn't mean that there are no new truths to be discovered in a passage of Scripture, but it does mean that any new understandings will have to answer to the historic, consensual understanding of the passage. For example, based on the Catholic Principle it would be impossible to conclude that Jesus was merely a man and not the unique Son of God, or that the Trinity is an outdated idea, or that Mary Magdalene was Jesus' live-in girlfriend. If our study leads us to an interpretation different from the church's understanding over time, the Catholic

Principle requires that we back up and re-approach the passage with the humility to admit that the wisdom of the ages is probably better than ours.

God did not leave us in the dark about his plan for salvation, and neither does he hide his plan for how Christians are to live and conduct themselves. He gave us the Bible as our primary rule, and reason and tradition to help.

Bishop Holloway would have us believe that "because we are born this way" we are excused for our behavior. He is right in one way: we are born this way. But just because we are born sinners doesn't give us permission to call good what is evil (Isaiah 5:20). The good news is that, in spite of our environment and genes, Christians, infused with God's love and imputed with God's righteousness, can choose over our sinful instincts to live according to God's plan, "because what the heart loves, the will obeys, and the mind justifies." [xxxvi]

Chapter 8

Crawling Out of Yourself

Anglicans have a unique and beautiful way of worshipping God that is based on the predictability of a Prayer Book service and the promise of meeting God in praise. It aims to appreciate God for who he is. Many are drawn to Anglican worship because it is Christ-centered, thoroughly biblical, and liturgically beautiful. Here are a few questions that newcomers to Anglican churches ask from time to time:

WHY DOES THE ANGLICAN CHURCH SEEM SO FORMAL?

It must seem formal to some, but the goal is to be "respectful," not formal. In fact there are formal Anglican churches (fancy vestments, organ music, etc.) and informal churches (blue jeans, guitars, etc.), but the common thread is a worship experience where we can crawl out of ourselves and into God. There we will have salve for our hurts, refreshment for our spirits and a "reset button" to put God back at the center of our lives. God lives everywhere, but he reveals his power and presence especially when Christians gather together in his name.

Anglicans are encouraged to prepare themselves to meet the Lord in worship. No one would casually and lackadaisically stroll into the office of the President of the United States or the Prime Minister of Canada; we would do so with the respect and dignity the office commands. In a similar way, Anglicans address God thoughtfully and with the utmost respect, with language that befits the Creator of the World, and King. Many pray when they first enter the church so that they can acknowledge Jesus' presence and Lordship – as you would acknowledge and greet the host when you first arrive at a dinner party.

Anglican worship challenges our selfish feed-*me*, coddle-*me*, entertain-*me* tendencies by pointing away from us – to God. Anglicans don't have to conjure up enthusiasm as we pray words that are bigger than the moment and prayers that are bigger than our emotions so as to draw us ever closer to God. The Rev. Dr. J. I. Packer said:

> "Slowly but surely, I became aware that Prayer Book services were celebrating the same realities that were shaping my life and from that point on the Prayer Book has anchored itself deeper and deeper in my conscious life." [xxxvii]

Holy Communion services begin with the words, "Blessed be God," not "Lord, *bless me*." This is notably different from the "bless me" attitude of the world and of many churches today. Some churches are *designed* to entertain and bless those who come – a filling station approach where the congregants go for one purpose: to get spiritually filled up for the week. But Anglicans focus on God; he's the audience; he's the reason why we come to pray and sing. Psalm 100 invites us to "enter his presence with thanksgiving; go into his courts with praise." We come to bless God with offerings (sacrifices) of praise and thanksgiving, the giving of our lives to him. We are spiritually filled when we don't seek to be filled, but when we lose ourselves and our needs in worship of the beauty of God.

What is one of our greatest blessings – a Christ-centered and thoroughly biblical liturgy – can also be our greatest curse. Familiarity and repetition can breed contempt, if we are not careful. Someone can say the words that for centuries have led people into the presence of God, but do it in a way that's mindless and never touches the heart. A parrot can be trained to recite the same words, but God is not impressed! There's a world of difference between a congregation that is captured by the majesty and wonder of God that is expressed so meaningfully in the Prayer Book, and one that is just going through the motions. Jesus' harshest criticism was reserved for the "religious" people of his day who, he said, "worship me with their lips, but their hearts are far from me" (Matthew 15:8). Anglicanism at its best has nothing to do with formalism and everything to do with the things that promote a heart-felt encounter with the living God. However mysterious and formal it may seem, all that we do in worship is meant to promote a sense of the greatness of God and the wonderful privilege of "entering his presence with thanksgiving."

AM I CRAZY OR DOES ANGLICAN WORSHIP FEEL "CATHOLIC"?

There's a historical reason for why Anglican worship has a Catholic flavor. Like all Protestant churches, we came from the Catholic Church in the 16th Century. The teaching of the medieval church (i.e., tradition) had acquired a sense of being the highest authority, and the Bible was viewed as subordinate – as one part of tradition. This allowed the church in the Middle Ages to subscribe to some extra-biblical and unbiblical teachings and practices. But when the Church of England broke from Rome and rediscovered the Bible as its highest authority, we began to test the traditions of the church against the teaching of Holy Scripture. Unlike some other Protestant churches that discarded everything "Catholic" in order to start a totally new thing, the Church of England didn't throw the baby out with the bathwater. The English Settlement reflects the conscious decision to retain the Catholic practices and traditions that don't conflict with the teaching of Holy Scripture. The result is a church that continues to have a "Catholic" flavor, but is thoroughly Protestant (i.e. biblical) in its teaching.

WHY DON'T YOU JUST SAY YOUR PRAYERS? WHY DO YOU READ THEM?

Anglicans are encouraged to talk to God often and in different ways. The Bible describes God as a friend (John 15:15) and we are invited to pray with the familiarity of a son talking to his father ("When you pray, say, 'Our Father . . .'"). Sometimes it is appropriate to pray spontaneous or extemporaneous prayers. Sometimes we use the tried and tested prayers of our Anglican tradition.

When Anglicans worship *corporately* we often use a form and prayers from the Prayer Book. It's our way of guaranteeing that everything in worship is done "decently and in order" (1 Corinthians 14:40). The first Book of Common Prayer was published in 1549 and the second in 1552. Thomas Cranmer, the first Archbishop of Canterbury of the Church of England, authored both. Since then there have been other revisions, all of them based on the rule: periodic change is necessary and good as long as the revisions remain faithful to the teaching of Holy Scripture (1789 Preface).

Every church has rituals and structure, even the so-called "non-liturgical churches." In fact they can be as structured about their non-structure as we are about our structure! Anglican worship is based on several important affirmations. First, that corporate Sunday worship is the most meaningful when worshippers have said their personal daily prayers between Sundays. The Anglican ideal is that every church member will pray the daily offices of Morning Prayer and Evening Prayer as found in the Book of Common Prayer.[xxxviii] Personal daily prayer and corporate worship are not substitutes one for the other – both are necessary for Christian growth. Also, some Anglicans find it helpful to come five or ten minutes early to church to quiet themselves and to prepare their hearts to receive from God. Many also find it helpful to read the Bible lessons appointed for the day before they come so that they are primed to hear God's Word.

Second, we frame our Sunday worship in the words that Christians throughout history have found helpful in expressing their concerns to God. This not only insures continuity to our theological tradition, it also keeps us from the kind of shallow individualism of prayers that are sometimes prayed from Protestant pulpits. Theologian Paul Zahl said,

> "We use a book because the inherited wisdom of the past is often more trust-worthy than the moods and opinions of the present moment. Yes, we desire our

prayers to breath conviction and humility. But we would not wish our prayers to be formed by whatever is just passing through our heads." [xxxix]

Prayer Book prayers are some of the most beautiful literary treasures in the English language, and they are rich in theological content and meaning. When we pray these prayers we pray in concert with those who have prayed them over the centuries (this is called "The Communion of Saints"). The Bible tells us that there is continual praise and worship in Heaven (Revelation 4, 5). This means that when we worship, our prayers and praises join with those already in progress in heaven.

And lastly, Anglicans affirm that worship is everyone's business, not just a minister on stage saying prayers for us. We see this especially in the responses that are invited from the congregation: e.g., "And also with you," "And blessed be his kingdom," "We lift them up to the Lord." The word "liturgy" literally means "the work of the people." The minister's job is not to entertain the troops or dazzle the crowds but to lead the congregation into the presence of the great and awesome God. It's every Christian's responsibility to contribute to worship by coming with prepared and expectant hearts, ready to give their voices and lives to God in singing and praying. When Christians make the prayers that the faithful have powerfully prayed over the centuries their own personal prayers, when the words of their songs truly express the singing in their hearts, and when they come with confidence that they will meet the Risen Lord, they experience this: "In your presence there is fullness of joy; in your right hand are pleasures forevermore!"(Psalm 16:11).

WHY IS IT CALLED "THE HOLY EUCHARIST?"

Anglicans worship in a variety of ways, including Morning and Evening Prayer services and the Holy Eucharist. All have long and respected places in corporate worship. What Anglicans call "The Eucharist" is called different things by different churches (the Divine Liturgy, the Lord's Supper, the Mass, etc.). The full title of the ACNA Holy Communion service is: "The Order for the Administration of The Lord's Supper or Holy Communion, commonly called the Holy Eucharist."

"Eucharist" is the English equivalent of the Greek word for "thanksgiving," and it's the most ancient term for what we do. This one word encapsulates the essence of Christian worship: we offer "humble thanks for all your goodness and loving-kindness to us and to all whom you have made..." (The General Thanksgiving, ACNA Liturgy for Morning Prayer).

There are two parts to the Holy Eucharist service: the Liturgy of the Word and Holy Communion – word and sacrament. History explains why we have this structure. The Bible tells us the first Christians were Jews and when they first believed in Jesus as the Messiah there was no reason to stop the practice of attending synagogue worship on the Sabbath (Saturday). In addition, on the day of the Lord's resurrection (Sunday), they also met to observe the celebration of Holy Communion that Jesus commanded: ("Do this in remembrance of me" (1 Corinthians 11). These two observances continued roughly until the Romans destroyed Jerusalem in the year A.D. 70. Christians were then forced to leave Jerusalem, providing the occasion to bring into one Sunday worship experience the elements of the Saturday synagogue worship (i.e., the word) and the Sunday observance of Holy Communion (i.e., the sacrament). The Liturgy of the Word is made up of the same elements as the Jewish synagogue service: prayers, readings from Holy Scripture, a sermon, and an offering. And Holy Communion is the distinctly "Christian" part, using bread and wine to celebrate Jesus' real presence in our lives. Where some denominations focus mostly on the Word (the many Protestant churches where the sermon is the focal point), and others on Holy Communion (Roman Catholics and Orthodox where the communion meal is often more important than the sermon), Anglicans acknowledge and honor both the word and the sacrament.

The two parts of our worship are bridged in some Prayer Books by what is called "The Peace" – when the congregation stands to greet one another with the words, "the peace of the Lord be with you." The Peace symbolizes our commitment to Christian love and forgiveness that is the foundation for Christian community. Jesus said that if you come to worship and there remember that someone has something against you, first go to be reconciled and then come back to make your offering (Matthew 5:23). At this point in the service, having obtained peace with God through confession of sins, we then proclaim and demonstrate our peace with one another. The Peace is a solemn prayer and blessing that we pray for one another. It is far more than a prelude to social hour or a way to get the kids into church from Sunday school. In the early church, new Christians studied for many months, sometimes years, before they could be baptized. In those days, people who were not yet baptized were dismissed with The Peace because only baptized Christians could participate in the Lord's Supper. Today Holy Communion is still reserved for Christians, who wish to renew their relationship with Jesus Christ.

Anglicans worship God in a variety of ways, from times of private prayer and praise to Morning and Evening Prayer and corporate Sunday worship. But the one common factor each time we worship is that we purpose to respect the amazing privilege it is to meet the King of kings and the Lord of lords!

Chapter 9

The Sacrament of New Birth

If someone from another planet were to visit an Anglican Church and observe infant baptism or a communion service, his journal entry might read:

> "How odd! Some kind of sadistic washing: parents smile dotingly while their baby suffers under cold water. And what looks like bread and wine is eaten, sometimes with tearful appreciation, by people who apparently think this is someone's body and blood! Strange people, these Anglicans!"

Strange as it must sound to some, Anglicans believe that God reveals himself in the Sacraments of the Church. The word "sacrament" comes from the Latin word meaning "pledge." These are more than mere symbols, they come with God's pledge, his promise, to deliver what they symbolize. They deliver the free and life-changing love of God (they are "effectual signs of Grace . . . towards us" Article XXV). God works in many different ways in the world, but one way that comes with a promise is the sacraments. Theologian Donald Bloesch says,

"Sacraments announce that Jesus is present; faith receives and acclaims this presence; faith working through love demonstrates and manifests this presence to the world." [xl]

We give the name "sacrament" primarily to Baptism and to Holy Communion, "the two sacraments ordained by Christ, which are generally for our salvation " (*To Be A Christian, An Anglican Catechism*, Q&A 104). These hold preeminence over other sacramental rites because Jesus Christ personally commanded their observance ("go therefore and make disciples, baptizing . . ." (Matthew 28), and "do this [Holy Communion] in remembrance of me" (1 Corinthians 11).

WHAT DOES BAPTISM DO?

Baptism is called the "sacrament of new birth." Since sacraments announce Jesus' presence, does this mean that becoming a Christian is the same thing as being baptized? Or does spiritual birth happen before, after, or quite apart from baptism? The experience of new birth, as it is described in the Bible, has two sides: God's gift and the receiving of the gift – what God does and what we do. Baptism is God acting towards us, not us towards him.[xli] For the grace extended to us in baptism to cause in us what God intends, it must be received by faith. Believing God and entering the new life sometimes begins before and sometimes after baptism. Faith is not something we do to earn God's love; it is simply surrendering to his love for us, and trusting him for salvation based what Jesus has accomplished for us on the cross (cf. John 1:12; Romans 10:9,13). Theologian and evangelist Michael Green says,

> "Baptism is the pledge of God's new life. But it is like a seed: it only germinates when it encounters the water of repentance and sunshine of faith … Baptism puts you into Christ, if you let yourself be put."[xlii]

For example, someone could give you a wrapped present, but unless you open it and discover the gift inside you don't have a clue what its value is or have any appreciation of its significance. It's a ridiculously sad thought, but someone could conceivably go through their whole life with the gift in their hands and never open it. This describes some who were baptized as infants but have never really entered the Kingdom of God that is prayed for in baptism and available to them by faith. They haven't lived into their baptisms and, in biblical terms, they are not saved.[xliii]

When someone is baptized in the name of the Father, and of the Son, and of the Holy Spirit the church in prayer asks God to give them the abundant life (John 10:10). Specifically we pray for the forgiveness of sins (1 Peter 3:21), for those who are joined with Christ in his death to be made alive with him in his resurrection (Romans 6:3,4), for them to cross from the kingdom of self into the kingdom of

God (Colossians 1:13,14), for spiritual birth (John 3:5), and that the newly baptized will be an active member of the church (1 Corinthians 12:13). God gives these graces to the baptized and, if they are met by faith, the baptized becomes alive to God in these ways and is saved (Romans 10:13). But if the baptized are too young to understand or if they don't respond in faith, God's grace does not automatically – i.e., *ex opere operato* – effect what these graces symbolize. As the Bible teaches, someone is not spiritually alive (i.e., born again) until he or she personally receives God's gift of salvation. Anglicans have always believed that the grace given in the sacraments is effective in our lives when, and only when, it is met by personal faith – "they that receive Baptism rightly . . ." (Article XXVII). "To all who received him, who believed in his name, he gave power to become children of God" (John 1:12).

WHY NOT RE-BAPTIZE?

Many Anglicans and others who were baptized as infants have been lulled into thinking that baptism is enough. They have experienced the "outward sign" of baptism but haven't yet lived into the reality of the *inward grace*. They have been baptized but are not yet spiritually reborn. My favorite image for this is "the man on an ox looking for an ox."[xliv] There he sits, heading off across the countryside looking for what is there the whole time. It's a pitiful picture if you think about it, but it describes the life of everyone who fails to live into his or her baptism by faith. The Apostle Paul describes something similar in his letter to the Ephesians: he told them that they were blessed in Christ with every spiritual blessing in the heavenly places (1:3). "Every blessing" obviously means that nothing was held back. So what's the problem in Ephesus? They simply didn't know how blessed they were. Paul went on to pray that the "eyes of their hearts would be enlightened so that they may know . . ." (vv. 17-19). It's totally possible to be blessed and not know it – to have the outward sign without the inward grace. If you were baptized as a baby and now realize that you are not "born again" – and you want to be – the appropriate response is not to be "re-baptized." This would be an insult to the prayers that were prayed for you in baptism and an insult to God's goodness in already answering those prayers. The appropriate response would be to accept God's gifts and thank him for the inheritance that has been waiting for you from your baptism and, even before that, from the cross of Christ where he won our full salvation – to accept Jesus as your Lord and Savior, and begin the new life with Christ.

WHY BAPTIZE INFANTS?

Roman Catholics emphasize the objective reality of God's grace and treat baptism as always effecting the new birth it symbolizes (the *ex opere operato* view of sacraments). Protestants generally emphasize personal conversion and they treat baptism only as a symbol of the new life that God gave them when they were converted. Anglicans hold a middle ground between these views. We believe that God objectively extends his grace in baptism, that it is far more than just a symbol. But to access the grace of baptism requires a personal response of faith, which itself is a gift from God.

So, if sacramental grace remains an unopened present until it's opened by faith, why not hold off on baptism until a person is old enough to make a personal decision for Christ? Anglicans, of course, baptize adults who have made an informed decision to follow Jesus as Lord. We also baptize babies when their Christian parents come before the church wanting their children to experience the fullest of God's blessings. Anglicans do this for several reasons:

1. Becoming a Christian and the rite of baptism are two very different things that are always separated by time. Baptism either precedes or follows the experience of conversion (i.e., repentance and personally accepting God's gift of salvation), but Christ commands us to do both. All the references to baptism in the Bible emphasize God acting towards us, not us toward him.

2. God loves children. Jesus accepted and blessed children too young to respond, and the Bible says that children don't need conversion to become like adults; rather, adults need conversion to become like children (Mark 10:13-16). The New Testament suggests that children were included among the families who were baptized together (Acts 2:39; 16:5, 32, 34), though this can't be proved one way or the other.

3. Circumcision, baptism's antecedent in the Old Testament, was performed on Jewish boys eight days old as a pledge and promise of Covenant blessings. This was obviously long before they could decide for themselves, yet circumcised babies were considered full members of the faith community. In the same way, baptism brings us into full membership in the New Covenant community (Colossians 2:11.12).

4. From the earliest Christians until Anabaptists questioned the practice of infant baptism in the 16th Century – for the first 1,500 years of Christendom! – it was the universal practice of the church to baptize infants. [xlv]

5. Lastly, and most important of all, infant baptism is the best example there is of God's unconditional love. It's the perfect picture of grace. Obviously, a three-month-old can't do anything to contribute to or earn his or her salvation, much less accept Jesus as their Savior. But God gives them the

gift of new life anyway. Before we loved him, he loved us (1 John 4:10). No one is saved because they deserve it or have earned it, but only because God freely gives it. Long before we knew God's love, he died on the cross for our sins. So why baptize infants? Because there's no reason to withhold from them the greatest gift of all. There's no reason not to welcome them into the community of believers who will love them into loving Jesus.

For all the reasons cited, Holy Baptism is far more than a social event or "having your child done." What happens in baptism has eternal consequences. For this reason, parents who bring their younger children for baptism should show by their commitment to worship every Sunday and to be involved in the ministry that they are serious about bringing their child up in the faith and life of the church. They should also choose godparents (called "Sponsors" in the Prayer Book) for their love of Jesus Christ and their willingness to help teach their child to know and love the Lord.

Our space alien visitor might be shocked, but for Anglicans sacraments announce the free gift of new life in Christ. They announce that God is present! In the next chapter we will take a look at another sacrament: that strange Christian eating ritual – and here I'm not talking about any church potluck.

Chapter 10

Cannibalism and Anglican Etiquette

I see a lot of different things as I distribute Holy Communion. Besides the humorous experiences of dropping the bread in awkward places and navigating around ladies hats and young children, I regularly see tears of joy and relief. A Sunday doesn't go by that I don't see someone who is deeply moved because through the sacrament of Holy Communion they have connected in a deep way with the Creator of the universe.

The word "Communion" comes from "common union," which might suggest that Holy Communion would be a focus for Christian unity. In fact, disagreements about the meaning of the Lord's Supper have caused more debates in the church than almost anything else. When Jesus said, "This is my body . . . this is my blood," did he mean his actual flesh and blood? Or, was he speaking poetically like when he said, "I am the door" or "I am the good shepherd?" So, what is the meaning of this strange eating ritual and why is it so important to Anglicans?

HOLY COMMUNION

"Sacraments announce that Jesus is present; faith receives and acclaims this presence . . . " [xlvi] God's part in Holy Communion is to show up (real presence). Our part is to receive him and be refreshed in the Holy Spirit as we eat the bread and drink the wine. On the night before he died, Jesus took the ordinary bread and wine of the Passover meal and assigned to them new meaning:

> "This is my body which is given for you. Do this in remembrance of me . . . this is the new covenant in my blood. Do this, as often as you drink it, in remembrance of me." (Matthew 26:26-28; Mark 14:22-24; Luke 22: 17-20)

He said two things: "this is my Body/Blood" and "do this in remembrance of me." These two assertions correspond to the two different ways Holy Communion has been understood in history. Roman Catholics focus almost exclusively on the first understanding. Thomas Aquinas, the 13th Century theologian, developed an elaborate explanation for the "real presence of Christ" that continues to dominate Catholic theology. Transubstantiation, as it's called, is the teaching that the bread and wine of Communion become the actual body and blood of Christ even though it still appears to be bread and wine. And the sacrifice of Jesus on the cross, Aquinas believed, is relived on the altar every time Holy Communion is celebrated.[xlvii] Not only does this theory explain how it happens, but also when and how. From an Anglican perspective, Transubstantiation leaves little to mystery, and it detracts from the biblical teaching that Jesus was sacrificed once for all (Heb. 9:28).

Many Protestants, on the other hand, focus on the "remembrance" part. They see Communion as a symbolic meal and the occasion to remember the events of the Last Supper and the Crucifixion. As Jews each year celebrate God's deliverance from Egypt (i.e., the Passover), so Jesus instituted Holy Communion to be a constant reminder that he delivered us from the bondage of sin by his sacrifice on the cross. Holy Communion, then, is the opportunity to renew a relationship with God who is spiritually present.

Anglicans generally represent a middle way between Catholics and, say, Baptists. Like Catholics, we believe that God is really present in the communion meal. But, unlike Catholics, we don't attempt to explain how it happens, when it happens, and what form it takes. Like the Baptists, we see Holy Communion as a time to remember what Jesus did and an opportunity for spiritual renewal. But unlike the Baptists, we believe that it is far more than a memorial meal – that Jesus meant it when he said "This is my body . . . this is my blood."

The middle way held by Anglicans between "Transubstantiation" and a "memorial supper" is seen in the words of administration in the first three Prayer Books. When the priest distributed bread using the first Book of Common Prayer (1549) he said, "The body of our Lord Jesus Christ" – suggesting a "real presence" understanding. The words were changed for the 1552 revision to: "Take them in remembrance" – suggesting a "memorial supper" understanding. And, in the 1559/1662 revisions, the Prayer Books that became the standard for many years, both sentences (and both ideas) were brought together:

> "The body of our Lord Jesus Christ which was given for thee, preserve thy body and soul unto everlasting life; take and eat them in remembrance that Christ died for thee, and feed on him in thy heart by faith with thanksgiving."

These are the words of administration that are used in the current ACNA Holy Communion service

As with every sacrament, the grace of Holy Communion is effective when it is faithfully received ". . . (by) such as rightly, worthily, and with faith, receive the same" (Article XXVIII). We recognize the importance of feeding on him in our hearts ". . . by faith with thanksgiving." Since receiving Holy Communion is about receiving God's very life, it is important to prepare oneself for Holy Communion. Paul wrote, "Whoever, therefore, eats the bread or drinks the cup of the Lord in an unworthy manner will be answerable for the body and blood of the Lord" (1 Corinthians 11:27). He goes on in the next verse to say, "Examine yourselves." This doesn't mean that we have to be perfect to come to the Lord's Table, only that we are aware of our need and ready to receive God's grace and mercy. Every Christian wishing to meet Jesus in the sacrament and be refreshed in his presence is welcome to receive.

THE NEW TESTAMENT TEACHES US SEVERAL THINGS ABOUT HOLY COMMUNION

First, coming to Communion is not an optional, take-it-or-leave-it experience for Christians. Jesus Christ commanded his followers "do this in remembrance of me." He never made such a command for Bible study, or prayer, or committee meetings. It is obviously a priority for Jesus that we continue this observance as a central feature of our corporate life.

Second, in Holy Communion we look forward to the day that Jesus will come again – when there will be a great heavenly banquet! "Truly I tell you," Jesus said at the Last Supper, "I will never again drink of the fruit of the vine until that day when I drink it new in the kingdom of God" (Mark 14:25). St. Paul likewise instructs us to continue to celebrate Holy

Communion until Jesus comes back (1 Corinthians 11:26). Communion is a foretaste of heaven in a day when few people give much thought to life after death or have much hope for heaven. The most obvious reason the first Christians were so excited and joyful was because they really believed that Jesus was coming back any day. They were anxious to experience the final installment of the Kingdom of God. Our experience as Christians is either rote and anemic or alive and vibrant – directly proportional to how much hope we have for heaven. Holy Communion proclaims that Jesus will one day come back to establish his kingdom forever: "Christ has died; Christ is risen; Christ will come again" (p. 363). It reminds us that Christ in us is "the hope of glory!" (Colossians 1:27).

Third, Communion reminds us that the church is central to God's plan. "Because there is one bread, we who are many are one body, for we all partake of the one bread" (1 Corinthians 10:17). We are born again, not in isolation, but into a Christian family. I laughed when I first saw the bumper sticker: "Lord, save me from your followers." Anyone who has been ambushed by pushy Christians or victimized by vulgar evangelism can empathize with the saying. However, its message falsely suggests that someone can be a growing and healthy Christian and not be in the church that Jesus Christ started and heads. No church is perfect and there are hypocrites in every one of them. Maybe many! But the church is God's idea and his plan for growing Christians (Ephesians 3:10). Holy Communion reminds us *where* we are spiritually nourished.

And lastly, and most wonderful of all, when we "feed on him in [our] hearts by faith" (p. 365) we feed on Jesus himself. He comes into us and dines with us (Revelation 3:20); he makes his home in us (John 14:23). As St. Paul said, "The cup of blessing that we bless, is it not a sharing in the blood of Christ? The bread that we break, is it not a sharing in the body of Christ?" (1Corinthians10:16). Holy Communion is renewing the intimacy with Jesus that is our birthright as his children – to be "filled with thy grace and heavenly benediction, and made one body with him, that he may dwell in us and we in him" (1979 Book of Common Prayer, p. 336).

The post-Communion prayers remind us that we are fed for a purpose. We are blessed in order to be a blessing to the world. In Holy Communion we are newly empowered for our most important ministry: to be God's witnesses. Although the sacrament offers us much comfort, consolation, and healing, its final purpose is to make us strong for God – in our families, neighborhoods, and workplaces. "And now, Father, send us out to do the work you have given us to do . . ."

In the next chapter we will examine other means of receiving God's grace besides the sacraments.

Chapter 11

Sign on the Dotted Line

I was taught in seminary to preach to felt-needs by checking each sermon for: *what are you asking them to do?* It made sense at the time because it kept my sermons fairly focused and it gave the flock something to work on. Sometimes it was "PRAY MORE." Often it was "GIVE MORE" or "DO MORE FOR GOD." Other times it was instruction about how to have a happy marriage. In the best of these sermons parishioners carried home with them some advice that might help in their daily lives.

Sounds good, right?

But the end result of all those years of try-harder do-more sermons was a congregation that, were they to be honest, felt beat up and inadequate because they never measured up. They could never do enough (I could never do enough!). Every week it was something else they had to do! *I was preaching law, not grace.* I was telling wonderful, spiritually-eager people what they should do for God, instead of what God has done for them in Jesus Christ. I shoulda-ed and oughta-ed them to upright Christian behavior. I was a nice man telling nice people to be nicer.

All the while I missed the point, and missed the opportunity. Christianity is not about a relationship with law but with a person. Jeremiah spoke of a New Covenant, one that would be coming six centuries later, in which people would love God and the law would move from writing on stone tablets to writing on human hearts (31:31). Jesus inaugurated the New Covenant by announcing the present reality of the Kingdom of God – it's at hand! He lived the perfect life that we can't possibly live, fulfilling the law when we couldn't (Matthew 5:17). He is the "end" of the law for righteousness (Romans 10:4). "God has done what the law, weakened by the flesh, could not do." (Romans 8:3). Jesus Christ redefined law and commandments from being "prescriptive" – a ladder to climb to get to God – to being "descriptive," i.e., describing what our lives will look like when we are rightly aligned with God. The law is good because it uncovers the truth of our utter inadequacy and our need for a Savior. But the heart of Christianity is a personal relationship with Jesus Christ.

So then, what about all the shoulds and oughts of prayer, Bible reading, faithful church membership, sacrificial giving, witnessing to others, etc.? Do we throw them out the window since we are no longer under law? Well, yes. If you throw them out they will come back, but with a right motive. You see, if we love Jesus Christ with all our heart, soul and mind, if we are really deeply in love with him as he is with us, then (with the right motive) we will naturally do all those things that grow our relationship. If you are not "doing" the things that will grow you spiritually, it's not a doing problem, it is a *love* problem. The Christian disciplines, and the celebration of disciplines, are helpful to be sure, not to reach God, but to grow in God who has already reached us.

If you look at Christians who have a joyful, dynamic and growing relationship with Jesus Christ, you will see that, almost to a person, they have these qualities:

THEY HAVE A DAILY TIME TO MEET WITH GOD

There is not one right way to read the Bible or pray. In fact, there are probably as many ways to meet God as there are people. But every Christian that I know who is growing deeper with God, whose faith and relationship has not lost energy and excitement, meets with God for prayer and Bible reading every day.

My dad was a lifelong churchman who was late coming to faith in Christ. He died 30 years ago, but my most vivid memory of him was as a child waking up for school at 5:30 or 6:00 always to find him reading the Bible in his La-Z-Boy recliner in the family room. He knew how important this is and he modeled it for his children.

Spending time with God brings us into the neighborhood where his grace and truth live. Reading the Bible for a few minutes or a few hours speaks to us the story of God's salvation in history and invites us into it, to be part of it. And not just reading, but praying the scriptures brings it home and applies it in life-changing ways to our own lives. Some find it a blessing to follow an Anglican lectionary (daily reading plan), others use plans to read through the Bible in a certain number of days and months. Some dig deeply into a verse or two for study and meditation; others read (or have read to them or listen to recordings) of larger portions of Scripture. For the sake of maintaining interest over the years I have found it helpful to periodically change up my "plan" over the years.

Praying is thanking God for who he is and telling him what is on our minds. It's conversation with the God who made us for friendship and relationship. It is asking him for things, but, more than that, it is aligning one's self with his purposes. Sometimes we speak, sometimes listen; sometimes we just sit as his feet enjoying his peaceful company. Some find it enriching to pray the Lord's Prayer slowly, phrase-by-phrase. Some keep prayer lists. Some have discovered the beauty of reading Morning Prayer or Evening Prayer in the Book of Common Prayer. In fact, "as important as it was (to Thomas Cranmer, the 16th Century author of the first Prayer Books) to get the Bible and the liturgy into the language of the people, it was equally important to get the monastic/cathedral pattern of constant (seven or eight-fold) prayer into the lives and families of Anglicans through the genius of a simplified pattern of praying with the rising and the setting of the sun."

Other disciplines that some have found helpful include memorizing portions of scripture, fasting from food (or, say, TV or the internet) to heighten concentration on God, or singing hymns (especially the old hymns with deep and profound theology), and/or reading spiritually uplifting books. For example, my spiritual life would be markedly poorer had I not read John Piper's *Desiring God*, Paul Zahl's *Grace in Practice*, Thomas Merton's *Contemplative Prayer*, Leo Tolstoy's *Father Sergius*, C.S. Lewis's *The Lion, the Witch and the Wardrobe*, and Steve Brown's *A Scandalous Freedom*.

So why do growing Christians meet with God every day? Because it's their duty or an obligation? No. Because their rector told them they should? Heck no. Compelled to by guilt or by some warped sense of penance? No! We read Scripture, pray and study because he who first called us into relationship also calls us into communion and friendship (John15:15). If we are enjoying the practice of meeting with God every day, it is because he first invited us to this intimacy. We love because he first loved us. (1John 4:19).

THEY ARE OUTWARDLY FOCUSED

Christians – who understand that it is not what we do for God that matters, but what God has done for us – know that we are blessed so that we can be a blessing to others and to the world. They know that there are not two classes of Christians: ministers that minister and congregations that congregate. They gladly use their time, talent and treasure to help others in Christian service and ministry. And the deeper they understand and internalize God's undeserved love, the more they will give themselves away for those who hurt.

It was said of miners during the California gold rush that they couldn't strike a vein of gold without the whole town knowing it. Their joy spontaneously spilled over into every aspect of their lives whether they wanted it to or not. The same is true of grace-rich Christians. Because they have received God's unearned love, they love lavishly. They naturally share their faith, both speaking about God in order to address the spiritual hunger others feel when they are apart from God, and taking action to address the physical needs they encounter in hurting people, close to home and far away. These are the two sides of Christian mission.

God's method for evangelism is not some arm-twisting plan or campaign. It is simply this: *beauty*. His plan is to build in us the beauty of his character and then send us into the world to stir up curiosity for God. Christians who live in God and whom God lives in are the hardest working employees, the most giving neighbors, and the best friends. The Bible says we are light in darkness. It will be evident in the kind way we treat the checkout clerk at the grocery story, in the bridges we build with neighbors through hospitality, by praying for those who do not yet know the love of God, and by our commitment to help the poor here and around the world. As opportunities open, we are eager to share how our story intersects with God's story, and how knowing him as Lord and Savior has changed our lives.

THEY ARE COMMITTED TO A LOCAL CHURCH

Those who have experienced the love of God and want to grow in that love are committed to a local church – and not just one toe in, but in the whole way! *Why?*

They know that they are born again, born not into a private, individualistic faith, but into community – the body of Christ, the family of God.

Church, over my lifetime, has gone from being the place/building where everyone simply went on Sunday mornings (for sometimes dubious social, religious and business reasons) to being recognized for what it truly is: a community of people who see the gathering of God's people as God's instrument to reach the world. Church is God's plan, his idea, for delivering his grace to his people and growing them into the people he wants them to be.

Christians commit to a local church knowing full well that they are joining a community of imperfect and broken people. It insults God to say, "I love God but hate the church" (That bumper sticker slogan again: "Lord, save me from your followers"). Church members know that Christian community is not easy. Churches are healthy when they upfront admit that every single member is a sinner and desperately needs the kind of love that God gives us – when the members extend grace to one another like God has extended his grace to us – when they have a habit of forgiving one another – and when their purpose is to find, grow and share the love of God in Jesus Christ the Lord.

The all too common practice of jumping ship for another church when the rector says something unpleasant or when the music doesn't agree with my personal preferences or when another church offers a more entertaining Sunday school for my children only disgraces "church" as God intended it. It hurts God's witness in the world. Families don't cease to be families when things don't go our way. Churches may grow by collecting disgruntled sheep from other folds, but the only growth that counts is when unchurched people see the church, its people, loving one another and supporting one another in good times and hard times. And when they see this they want to join a community of hope like that, whose identity is found in the character of Jesus Christ.

Church is not an optional extra for Christians. It is central to God's plan for the world. The author of Hebrews warned against "neglecting to meet together, as is the habit of some . . ." (10:25). Keeping the Sabbath holy (the 4th Commandment), at the very least, involves worshipping every Sunday with your church family. If you have children, this means maintaining a family tradition that "going to corporate worship and experiencing God in Christian community every week is what this family does." And all of this isn't because it is required or expected by your pastor or the law – but because you want to be where God is specially meeting his people in word and sacrament. The local church is where we learn to live into the implications of God's grace. It's His plan. It's his idea.

THEY ARE ACTIVELY INVOLVED WITH A SMALL GROUP OF CHRISTIAN FRIENDS

There's a world of difference between "going" to church and being the church. Some churches are large enough that one could attend for years and still be the loneliest, most insular Christian on the planet. Church is more than a building or a Sunday morning observance; it is a community to invest yourself in. Even if you attend church every Sunday, the fact is most spiritual growth occurs when Christians meet together in small groups to support and encourage one another. Jesus' whole ministry was given to a small group of twelve disciples. Small groups were the main structure of church for the New Testament Christians (Acts 2:46; 10:22; 12:12; 16:32; 20:7; 21:8).

There are about 60 "One Another" statements in the New Testament (love one another; building up one another; accept one another; admonish one another; challenging one another; etc.). They all point to the reality of close and deeply personal relationships. Such relationships simply do not happen when you see your fellow church members for an hour or two on Sunday mornings, especially since most of that time is spent listening to someone (a Sunday school teacher or preacher) talking at you.

This is a far cry from what Jesus had in mind when he established the church. Involvement in a small group can be the most important place where Christians grow from the Bible, pray for one another, encourage and pastor one another, and show the unbelieving world that it is the greatest joy to experience true Christian fellowship.

THEY ARE GENEROUS

It is impossible to be touched by the unlimited generosity of God and not eventually become ridiculously generous. Giving is the test. If you are a miserly, stingy person with your time, talent and treasure, pray that God's grace will take root in your heart. Pray that you will know the height and depth of his incredible love.

For years I taught and practiced tithing (10% before taxes for the church) as the minimum standard of Christian giving. There's no doubt that it is the law in the Old Testament (Malachi 3:8-12), and it was even the practice before Moses and the law (Genesis 14:17-20). But Old Testament "tithing" was a tax to support the religious and civil structures of Israel – a theocracy. The New Testament and the New Covenant have radically changed everything, including giving from law to giving from grace.

God wants *you*; he doesn't want your money. He is concerned about the condition of your heart and how giving can show that God is, in fact, your highest love. It is God's bubbling-up grace in your life that matters, not a response to an external command from the pulpit or a home-visit from a member of the capital funds campaign.

In 1 Corinthians 16:2 St. Paul instructs the church to take a weekly collection in which each person gives "as he may prosper." Christians are to give enough that it matters, that it impacts their lifestyles. To give much without sacrifice insults God who gave us everything. Giving "as the Lord prospers" doesn't mean going into debt or doing something stupid, but it may mean doing with smaller vacations or no vacation this year, buying a used car instead of a new one, or waiting a few years to fix the kitchen. The poor widow gave only a few cents, but it was everything she had – and she is remembered to this day for her complete love for God (Mark 12:41-44). C. S. Lewis once said,

> "If our charities do not at all pinch or hamper us I should say they are too small. There ought to be things we should like to do and cannot because our charitable expenditures exclude them." [xlviii]

For some giving 2% impacts their lifestyle and means something to them. For others it may be 75%.

Life under grace means that we don't give a certain percentage, but instead, we give in proportion to how blessed we are and in such a way that it cost us something. This means that, if we are saved for eternity, and if our real treasure is in heaven, our giving will be pure "thanksgiving." So many Christians can tell you that there is power and joy in tallying up their giving for the year and seeing how good God has been to them. God loved the world so much that he gave us everything, not even holding back his only begotten Son.

About the Author

Chuck Collins has written extensively for Christian journals and magazines on matters of theology and church history. He loves the Anglican heritage rooted in the Reformation's respect for the Bible as primary authority, in the early church fathers as initial interpreters of Scripture, and a reasoned and balanced view of Christian theology. Perhaps best known for his ten's years as Rector of Christ Church (Episcopal) in San Antonio, the largest church of its diocese, a church that had a reputation for strong biblical preaching and its commitment to outreach and mission.

Chuck is also an award-winning short story writer and poet, winning the 2013 *Writer's Digest* Annual Competition in the religious inspirational category for his short story *After a Long Spell*. Then winning the First Prize in the 2014 *Utmost Christian Writer's Foundation* Poetry Contest for his poem *New Day*.

"Great grace" (Acts 4:33) came upon Chuck when he was eighteen, bringing him literally to his knees one Sunday morning while watching a Baptist minister on TV. Working his way through college cleaning carpets, pumping gas, and cooking at a local steak house, he eventually graduated from the *University of Texas, El Paso* with a degree in philosophy. He holds a masters in theology (M.Div) from *Seminary of the Southwest* where during his first week he met Ellen, a student at the University of Texas. They fell in love and have been married 35 years, with four grown children and four grandchildren. Chuck has served churches in Florida, New Mexico and Texas and is now on staff at Christ Church Anglican, Phoenix, Arizona. He has been a retreat and conference speaker, a canon theologian, an instructor and trustee of Christian educational institutions, and Dean of the San Antonio CANA/ACNA Archdeaconry.

Chuck's passion in life is not to push people across the Salvation line, but to provoke people to consider the beauty and grace of God.

Ever a servant Chuck Collins has led dozens of missions and pilgrimages around the world, including many trips to Jordan and Israel.

Endnotes

[i] *Calvinism in the Las Vegas Airport* (Grand Rapids: Zondervan, 2004), p. 32.

[ii] A Hudson, "John Wyclif," *The English Religious Tradition and the Genius of Anglicanism*, ed. G. Rowell (Nashville: Abingdon, 1992), p. 76.

[iii] Cranmer reached Henry early in the morning, soon enough to ask the King if he would put his faith in Jesus Christ. Henry responded that he wanted to. "Cranmer had won a final victory in his years of argument with the King on justification." D. MacCulloch, *Thomas Cranmer: A Life* (New Haven: Yale Press, 1996), p. 360.

[iv] D. MacCulloch, *The Later Reformation in England, 1547-1603 (Second Edition)*, (Hampshire: Palgrave/Macmillan), p. 11.

[v] J.C. Ryle, *Five English Reformers* (Carlisle PA, Banner of Truth Trust, 1981), p. 22.

[vi] The term "Anglican" here is, strictly speaking, anachronistic. It was first used by John Henry Newman in 1838 and soon thereafter acquired the sense of "pertaining to the Church of England." Sykes and Booty (ed.), "Anglicanism," J.R Wright, *The Study of Anglicanism* (Minneapolis: Fortress, 1988), p. 424.

[vii] R. Prichard, *A History of the Episcopal Church* (Harrisburgh: Morehouse, 1991), p. 2.

[viii] There are 38 Autonomous Provinces that make up the Anglican Communion, of which the Episcopal Church is one.

[ix] C. Loveland, *The Critical Years: The Reconstitution of the Anglican Church in the United States of America: 1780-1789* (Greenwich CT: Seabury Press, 1956), p. 61.

[x] Other "irregular" consecrations have occurred in modern times, not least of which are the consecrations for the Anglican Mission in America in 2000. "Irregular," yes, but not without historic precedent.

[xi] Loveland, p. 284. Also David Summer, author of *The Episcopal Church's History 1945-1985* wrote: "Like most church leaders, I believed that the diocese was the primary unity of the Episcopal Church, and that its strength - compared with those 'Congregationalist churches' - was that we 'did things together'...I've changed my mind... The diocese exists to enable the ministry of the local congregation and not the other way around," "The Living Church" (June 9, 2002), p. 25.

[xii] N. Atkinson, *Richard Hooker: And the Authority of Scripture, Tradition and Reason* (Vancouver: Regent College Publishing, 1977), p. 130.

[xiii] The Caroline Divines [Taylor, Bull, Law] radically departed from the Reformation synthesis "and prepared the way for a moralism that has

afflicted English theology ever since and still afflicts it today, a moralism which is less than the full gospel." p. X; "Their remedy for sin consisted largely of exhortations to lead a holy life. Moreover, the only veritable significance attached to the atonement was the *moral* example of Christ," p. 192. C. F. Allison, *The Rise of Moralism: The Proclamation of the Gospel from Hooker to Baxter (Vancouver: Regent College Publishing, 1966).*

xiv C. Gore, ed. *Lux mundi: A Series of Studies in the Religion of the Incarnation,* 10th ed. (London: John Murray, 1890).

xv Harp's definition of the Broad Church movement of Phillips Brooks. G. Harp, *Brahmin Prophet: Phillips Brooks and the Path of Liberal Protestantism (New York: Rowman & Littlefield, 2003), p. 138).*

xvi Anglican House Publishers, Inc. ISBN 978-0-9860441-2-0

xvii "What Scripture doth plainly deliver, to that first place both of credit and obedience is due; the next whereunto is whatsoever any man can necessarily conclude by force of reason; after these the voice of the Church succeedeth. That which the Church by her ecclesiastical authority shall probably think and define to be true or good, must in congruity of reason over-rule all other inferior judgments whatsoever." (*Laws*, Book V, 8:2, Folger Ed 2:39, 8-14).

xviii "A Stool or a Tower?" *The Anglican Digest* (Transfiguration 2005, vol. 47, no. 4), p. 11.

xix Seminary professor, Michael Floyd, exposes the *lex orandi* formula as a foreign idea to Anglicanism, and the three-legged stool as a "recent innovation, giving expression more to twentieth century ideas than to traditionally Anglican ones." "Are the Scriptures Still Sufficient?" *Our Heritage and Common Life,* ed. W. Adams and M. Floyd (Lanham MD: University Press of America, 1994). p. 49.

xx Clergy in the Church of England are required to acknowledge The Articles as that "which bear witness to the faith revealed in Scripture and set forth in the catholic creeds" (Canon C 15). William White, the first Presiding Bishop of the Episcopal Church, championed the Articles, but did not require their subscription in the U.S. since they were included in the Constitution of the Church, and everyone ordained vowed to uphold the doctrine and discipline of the Church (including the Constitution). The neglect of The Articles is surely one of the great tragedies of modern Anglicanism.

xxi "It doesn't occur to many people that what they call 'tolerance' is really sheer lack of conviction. It is not particularly significant if a man who has no great convictions says he is tolerant. Indeed, tolerance is a virtue only if a man believes something very strongly, yet respects the rights of others to disagree." L. Ford, *The Christian Persuader* (Minneapolis: World Wide Publications, 1988), p. 18.

xxii "When we set the two side by side - our heavy, weighty, monumental sin on one side of the balance, and the depth of God's love on the other side - the side of the scale holding love pounds resolutely on the foundations of the world and resounds throughout all ages." M.R. McMinn, *Why Sin Matters* (Wheaton: Tyndale, 2004), p. 17.

xxiii See also: Psalm 14: 2,3; Job 15:14; Jeremiah 17:9; Romans 5:12.

xxiv The Bible and Anglicans have a low anthropology and a high christology. "The lower we are made to go in knowing ourselves as sinners, the higher shall we rise in joy when assurance of God's pardon breaks in. To play down the sinfulness of sin is to obscure the greatness of grace." J.I. Packer quoted in Leuenberger, p. 276.

xxv S. Brown, *A Scandalous Freedom: The Radical Nature of the Gospel* (New York: Brown Simon & Schuster, 2004), p. 246.

xxvi P. Zahl, *Grace in Practice: A Theology of Everyday Life* (Grand Rapids: Eerdmans, 2007), p. 17.

xxvii L. Newbigin, *The Gospel in a Pluralistic Society* (Grand Rapids: Eerdmans, 1989), p. 21.

xxviii Additionally, the seven "I am" sayings in John's gospel clearly identify Jesus with the God of the Bible who stated that his name is "I am" in Exodus 3:14 (John 3:35; 8:12; 10:7; 11:25; 14:6; 15:1). "Jesus said to them, "very truly, I tell you, before Abraham was, I am" (John 8:58).

xxix *More Than One Way? Four Views on Salvation in a Pluralistic World* (Grand Rapids: Zondervan, 1995), p. 177.

xxx *The Great Divorce* (New York: Macmillan, 1978), p. 72.

xxxi Calvinists believe that atonement is limited because a sovereign God would not have failed to accomplish what he sets out to do in sending his only Son. Arminians limit atonement when they contend that salvation is not guaranteed for all persons for whom Christ died. Don't all Christians see that "our coming to faith has a strong element of being drawn in against our own inclinations?" R. Mouw, *Calvinism in the Las Vegas Airport* (Grand Rapids: Zondervan, 2004), p. 32.

xxxii R. Capon sermon "The Pharisee and the Publican."

xxxiii Attributed to N.T. Niles.

xxxiv Newbigin, p. 72.

xxxv *The Rebirth of Orthodoxy* (San Francisco: Harper Collins, 2003), p. 31.

xxxvi http://www.mbird.com/2011/01/ashley-null-via-thomas-cranmer

xxxvii In a conversation with Julie Lane-Gay, speaking about the significance of the Book of Common Prayer (1662) on its 350th birthday. On line "Anglican Planet": Saturday, November 4, 2012.

xxxviii Morning and Evening prayer in most Anglican prayer books reflects the intention of the reforming Archbishop of Canterbury Thomas Cranmer to return to the offices as the daily prayer of parish churches and parishioners.

xxxix *The Beacon*, Fall 1999, Trinity Episcopal School for Ministry.

xl *The Church: Sacraments, Worship, Ministry, Mission* (Downers Grove: InterVarsity, 2002), p. 175.

xli "Cranmer knew that sacraments were God's ways of working, not man's; that the only appropriate human response was one of reception, with the organ of faith, itself a gift of God." P. Collinson, "Thomas Cranmer," p. 95.

xlii *Baptism: Its Purpose, Practice and Power* (Downers Grove: InterVarsity, 1987), p. 56-57.

xliii A famous ecclesiastical trial in 1850 addressed the question of whether or not a person is reborn automatically (*ex opere operato*) when they are baptized. Henry Philpotts, the Anglican bishop of Exeter, refused to institute George Gorham as rector because he didn't believe that every baptized person is born again. Gorham won the case, and the Privy Council stated, "Grace may be granted before, in or after baptism...but only in such as worthily receive it."

xliv John Claypool, *The Preaching Event: Lyman Beecher Lectures* (Waco, TX: Word, 1980), p. 78.

xlv The one notable exception among the church fathers was Tertullian (160-220 AD). He objected to infant baptism, not on the grounds related to faithful reception, but because it "imposes too great a responsibility on the godparents; they might die and so be unable to fulfill their obligations." Green, p. 74.

xlvi Bloesch, p. 175.

xlvii For the entire history of Anglicanism the term "altar" was intentionally avoided in favor of "holy table" to show that Anglicans have a once-and-for-all understanding of the sacrifice of Christ. In the 1979 Book of Common Prayer "altar" was reintroduced into the rubrics of the Holy Communion service taking the Episcopal Church back to a pre-Reformation understanding of Holy Communion. Adding to the confusion was the addition of the fraction anthem which suggests a re-sacrifice on an altar: "Christ our Passover is sacrificed for us" - rather than "was sacrificed" (1 Cor. 5:7).

xlvii *Mere Christianity* (New York: Harper Collins, 2001), p. 87

Appendix A

We Really Do Believe in the Catholic Church

There is a much-misunderstood phrase in the creed that Anglicans recite every Sunday. Anglicans understand "catholic" in the same way it was originally intended, i.e. universal (not *Roman* Catholic). We are committed to the historic faith of the church that is sometimes called the "ancient consensual faith" or "traditional Christianity." And we are linked permanently to all others today and back to Jesus' time who believe the same thing. This passing-on of the teachings of Scripture is called Apostolic Succession, and it is symbolized in the laying on of hands from one bishop to the next in the consecration of new bishops.

Historian Owen Chadwick said that a 'catholic mind' is a Christian mind with a sense of Christian history.[i] The New Testament says that there is a body of unchanging truth passed on to each generation that connects us to the previous generations, all the

---

[i] *The Spirit of the Oxford Movement: Tractarian Essays* (Cambridge: Cambridge University Press, 1992), p. 308.

way back to the apostles (2 Timothy 2:2). Jude spoke of this as "the faith that was once and for all entrusted to the saints" (v. 3). Paul called it "the common faith" (Titus 1:4) and "the faith of the gospel" (Philippians 1:27). The Prayer Book calls it "the substance of the faith" (p. 9). ACNA's Catechism states, "The term 'catholic' means 'according to the whole.' The Church is called 'catholic' because it holds the whole faith once for all delivered to the saints, and maintains continuity with the Apostolic church throughout time and space" (Q&A 95). This is what it means to be "catholic."

Anglicans are obviously not Roman Catholic. In the early to late Middle Ages the Roman Catholic Church veered away from its original Scriptural foundations and formally adopted some extra-biblical and unbiblical beliefs. They manufactured theology supporting the infallibility of popes and doctrines that include transubstantiation, adoration of Mary the mother of Jesus, purgatory, indulgences, mandatory confession to a priest, and the practice of praying to the saints. Originally, the 16th Century reformers never wanted to leave the Catholic Church; they wanted to return it to its biblical foundations. "They never saw themselves as anything other than true Catholics who were simply returning to the authentic, original script for their centuries-old faith, the Bible."[ii] But the Church in Rome would not let them. Reformation's loyalty to the Bible and to the catholic faith was stronger than loyalty to the structure of the Catholic Church, and eventually Reformers chose to walk the path of catholic Christianity, even if it meant leaving the Roman Church behind.

Today there are Protestants who are quite Catholic in their beliefs and practices and Roman Catholics who are almost indistinguishable in their beliefs from Protestants. But there is the one big distinction of the Reformation – the huge looming issue – that still remains: How is someone saved (become righteous before God)? "Can mortal man be right before God? Can a man be pure before his Maker?" (Job 4:17).

Catholics – from the Middle Ages and the time of the Council of Trent (1545-1564) all the way to today – believe that someone is saved when they are righteous, innately righteous, through the grace of the sacraments, which is to say "we are OK *when* we become OK." Catholics define justification as a process of moral transformation that begins at baptism, increases through one's obedience, and (hopefully) yields a final justification at the end of one's life. Protestants, on the other hand, believe they

---

[ii] Ashley Null, "Thomas Cranmer and Tutor Evangelicalism," *The Advent of Evangelicalism: Exploring Historical Continuities*, ed. Haykin and Stewart (Nashville: B & H Academic, 2008), p. 227.

are never righteous enough in their own doings; therefore, they look to God and put their trust and faith in God's righteousness credited to their account – "we are OK *before* we actually become OK." Protestants believe that righteousness that justifies is never inherent within the believer, but is always the righteousness of another that renders the ungodly person just before a holy God. This is the difference between "infused righteousness" and "imputed righteousness."

Anglicans believe that righteousness is accorded Christians not because we become righteous but because God in his mercy has credited his own righteousness to us. Archbishop Thomas Cranmer "concluded that the medieval Catholic doctrine of salvation by increments did not spur a sinner to cling to God's grace even as he climbed the ladder of good works to heaven."[iii] "We do not presume to com to this thy Table, O merciful Lord, trusting in our own righteousness . . ." (p. 337). When God looks at us he doesn't see our *unrighteousness* ("No one is righteous, not even one." Romans 3:10), but he sees his Son who covers me with the robe of righteousness (Isaiah 61:10). Article XI of the Thirty-nine Articles states:

> "Man is very far gone from original righteousness, and is on his own nature inclined to evil, so that the flesh

---

[iii] Ashley Null, *Thomas Cranmer's Doctrine of Repentance: Renewing the Power to Love* (Oxford: Oxford University Press, 2006), p. 132.

lusteth always contrary to the Spirit; and therefore in every person born into this world, it deserveth God's wrath and damnation. And this infection of nature doth remain, yea in them that are regenerated."

The doctrine of imputed righteousness is found in certain passages of St. Paul, notably Romans 4: 6, 11, where Christians are "reckoned" to be righteous by the righteousness of Christ. Paul, writing the church in Philippi said, " . . . not having a righteousness of my own that comes from the law, but that which comes through faith in Christ, the righteousness from God that depends on faith" (3:9). The "gospel" is described by St. Paul as the righteousness of God and the power of God (Romans 1:16, 17).

Many Anglicans and Protestants could possibly overlook infallibility of the pope and the inordinate attention given to Mary, but can't get past the central biblical issue of how a person is saved. But just because someone is a convinced Protestant does not mean they speak from a place of superiority. No, just the opposite! Because we believe we are "not worthy so much as to gather up the crumbs under thy table" and that "this infection of nature doth remain," we are sinners whose only hope is the completed work of Christ on the cross for our salvation. Because we humbly receive what we don't deserve, we are humble and graceful towards those who do not believe as we do.

Appendix B

Canterbury Tales . . .

It is popular for Anglicans to define themselves in terms of their relationship to the Archbishop of Canterbury. For some to be "in communion with Canterbury" seems to be more important than maintaining continuity with historic Anglicanism and the teaching of Holy Scripture. In recent years Anglicans have seen the authority of the Archbishop of Canterbury balloon in stature from being *first among equals* (the other Anglican primates[iv] and bishops) to almost pope-like status. This constitutes a stunning shift in understanding from a theological identity to an institutional identity.

With uncanny foresight in 1948 the Lambeth Conference (decennial conference of worldwide Anglican Bishops) declared:

> "Former Lambeth Conferences have wisely rejected proposals for a formal primacy of Canterbury . . . authority which binds the Anglican Communion together is therefore seen to be moral and spiritual, resting on the truth of the Gospel, and on a charity

---

[iv] The Anglican Communion has 38 Provinces covering the globe, each led by a senior bishop, i.e. a "Primate."

which is patient and willing to defer to the common mind."[v]

The Primates of the Anglican Communion (the Archbishops of the 38 Anglican Provinces globally), also concerned about the exponential growth of Canterbury's power and influence, expressed this after their 2005 meeting in Dromantine, Ireland:

> "We also have further questions concerning the development of the role of the Archbishop of Canterbury, and (his) Council of Advice. While we welcome the ministry of the Archbishop of Canterbury as that of one who speaks to us as *primus inter pares* (first among equals) about the realities we face as a Communion, we are cautious of any development which would seem to imply the creation of an international jurisdiction which could override our proper provincial autonomy."[vi]

Even a recently retired Archbishop of Canterbury himself spoke of the overstated view of his own bishopric:

> "I think someone recently said that 'the path to heaven doesn't necessarily lie through Lambeth.' I agree entirely. The path to heaven lies solely through Jesus Christ our Savior and the unity he gives, and the

---

[v] *Resolutions of the Twelve Lambeth Conferences 1867-1988*, ed. Roger Coleman (Toronto: Anglican Book Centre, 1992), p. XIII-XIV.

[vi] "Primates Meeting Communique," Feb. 19, 2007, *www.episcopalchurch.org/3577_82571_*.

only use and integrity of the instruments of unity [including the Archbishop of Canterbury] is hen they serve that."[vii]

Seminary professor William Witt, in a brilliant essay on this topic, pointed out that there are no references to the See of Canterbury in any of the classical Anglican writings (including the Articles of Religion and the Book of Common Prayer). He concluded that,

> "If one actually reads Cranmer or Jewel or Hooker et al, it becomes quite clear that (as they broke with Rome) they would have had no hesitation to break with Canterbury should Canterbury break with the doctrines and practices which encapsulate the gospel – because the identity of Anglicanism does not lie in communion with an historic see, but in the doctrines and practices that adhere to the gospel."[viii]

All Anglicans agree that Canterbury is an historic see and the Archbishop of Canterbury is the symbolic head of the Anglican Communion, but to give him the kind of extraordinary authority over the church that he currently enjoys distorts what Anglicans have historically believed. Anglicans have consistently said

---

[vii] Quoted in Michael Nai-Chiu Poon, "Farewell to Babel: Rowan Cantuar as servant of unity for the one, holy, catholic and apostolic Communion," 2006 essay on the Global South Anglican website.

[viii] "Is it Necessary to be in Communion with Canterbury to be Anglican?" Non Sermoni Res blog: *willgwitt.org.*

that the Archbishop of Canterbury's word is only as good as he upholds God's Word, and his authority only as strong as he upholds the Anglican heritage. To give our loyalty to a man or to an institution is, simply, misplaced loyalty. The 2008 Global Anglican Futures Conference (GAFCON), a meeting in Jerusalem of Anglican primates, bishops and clergy and lay leaders from around the world, got it right when they stated:

> "While acknowledging the nature of Canterbury as an historic see, we do not accept that Anglican identity is determined necessarily through recognition by the Archbishop of Canterbury. [ix]

Being "Anglican," therefore, means a theology, a heritage, something we believe - not an institution that we submit to."

The Archbishop of Canterbury cannot rescue Anglicanism from the storm it finds itself in with huge divisions caused when progressive theologies collide with orthodox Christianity. There are no political solutions to theological problems. Our real hope is what the Prayer Book calls "the substance of the faith," and what the Bible calls "the faith once and for all delivered to the saints." This, and only this, gives us direction and hope for the future of the Anglican Communion.

[ix] The Jerusalem Declaration, *www.gafcon.org.*

Appendix C

The Jerusalem Declaration

(Adopted June 28, 2008 in Jerusalem)

In the name of God the Father, God the Son and God the Holy Spirit:

We, the participants in the Global Anglican Future Conference, have met in the land of Jesus' birth. We express our loyalty as disciples to the King of kings, the Lord Jesus. We joyfully embrace his command to proclaim the reality of his kingdom which he first announced in this land. The gospel of the kingdom is the good news of salvation, liberation and transformation for all. In light of the above, we agree to chart a way forward together that promotes and protects the biblical gospel and mission to the world, solemnly declaring the following tenets of orthodoxy which underpin our Anglican identity.

1. We rejoice in the gospel of God through which we have been saved by grace through faith in Jesus Christ by the power of the Holy Spirit. Because God first loved us, we love him and as believers bring forth fruits of love, ongoing repentance, lively hope and thanksgiving to God in all things.

2. We believe the Holy Scriptures of the Old and New Testaments to be the Word of God written and to contain all things necessary for salvation. The Bible is to be translated, read, preached, taught and obeyed in its plain and canonical sense, respectful of the church's historic and consensual reading.

3. We uphold the four Ecumenical Councils and the three historic Creeds as expressing the rule of faith of the one holy catholic and apostolic Church.

4. We uphold the Thirty-nine Articles as containing the true doctrine of the Church agreeing with God's Word and as authoritative for Anglicans today.

5. We gladly proclaim and submit to the unique and universal Lordship of Jesus Christ, the Son of God, humanity's only Saviour from sin, judgement and hell, who lived the life we could not live and died the death that we deserve. By his atoning death and glorious resurrection, he secured the redemption of all who come to him in repentance and faith.

6. We rejoice in our Anglican sacramental and liturgical heritage as an expression of the gospel, and we uphold the 1662 Book of Common Prayer as a true and authoritative standard of

worship and prayer, to be translated and locally adapted for each culture.

7. We recognise that God has called and gifted bishops, priests and deacons in historic succession to equip all the people of God for their ministry in the world. We uphold the classic Anglican Ordinal as an authoritative standard of clerical orders.

8. We acknowledge God's creation of humankind as male and female and the unchangeable standard of Christian marriage between one man and one woman as the proper place for sexual intimacy and the basis of the family. We repent of our failures to maintain this standard and call for a renewed commitment to lifelong fidelity in marriage and abstinence for those who are not married.

9. We gladly accept the Great Commission of the risen Lord to make disciples of all nations, to seek those who do not know Christ and to baptise, teach and bring new believers to maturity.

10. We are mindful of our responsibility to be good stewards of God's creation, to uphold and advocate justice in society, and to seek relief and empowerment of the poor and needy.

11. We are committed to the unity of all those who know and love Christ and to building authentic ecumenical relationships. We recognise the orders and jurisdiction of those Anglicans who uphold orthodox faith and practice, and we encourage them to join us in this declaration.

12. We celebrate the God-given diversity among us which enriches our global fellowship, and we acknowledge freedom in secondary matters. We pledge to work together to seek the mind of Christ on issues that divide us.

13. We reject the authority of those churches and leaders who have denied the orthodox faith in word or deed. We pray for them and call on them to repent and return to the Lord.

14. We rejoice at the prospect of Jesus' coming again in glory, and while we await this final event of history, we praise him for the way he builds up his church through his Spirit by miraculously changing lives.

Appendix D

Ministry and Duties of ACNA Laity

Anglicans Church in North America

Canons Title I, Canon 10

Of the Laity

Section 1 - *Concerning Ministry*

The people of God are the chief agents of the Mission of the Church to extend the Kingdom of God by so presenting Jesus Christ in the power of the Holy Spirit that people everywhere will come to put their trust in God through Him, know Him as Savior and serve Him as Lord in the fellowship of the Church. The effective ministry of the Church is the responsibility of the laity no less than it is the responsibility of Bishops and other Clergy. It is incumbent for every lay member of the Church to become an effective minister of the gospel of Jesus Christ, one who is spiritually qualified, gifted, called, and mature in the faith. Each diocese may establish standards for the ministry of the laity.

Section 2 - *Concerning Duties of the Laity*

It shall be the duty of every member of the Church:

1. To worship God, the Father, and the Son and the Holy Spirit, every Lord's Day in a Church unless reasonably prevented;

2. To engage regularly in the reading and study of Holy Scripture and the Doctrine of the Church as found in Article I of the Constitution of this Church;

3. To observe their baptismal vows, to lead an upright and sober life, and not give scandal to the Church;

4. To present their children and those they have led to the Lord for baptism and confirmation;

5. To give regular financial support to the Church, with the biblical tithe as the minimum standard of giving;

6. To practice forgiveness daily according to our Lord's teaching;

7. To receive worthily the Sacrament of Holy Communion as often as reasonable;

8. To observe the feasts and fasts of the Church set forth in the Anglican formularies;

9. To continue his or her instruction in the Faith so as to remain an effective minister for the Lord Jesus Christ;

10. To devote themselves to the ministry of Christ among those who do not know Him, utilizing

the gifts that the Holy Spirit gives them, for the effective extension of Christ's Kingdom.

Section 3 - *Concerning Membership in the Church*

Membership in the Church requires that a person has received the Sacrament of Baptism with water in the Name of the Father, and of the Son, and of the Holy Spirit, and that such a person be accepted as a member of the Church by a congregation of this Church in compliance with the Constitution of the Church. Such a person is a baptized member of the Church. A confirmed member is a baptized member who has been confirmed or received by a Bishop of the Church.

Appendix E

The Articles Of Religion

I. Of Faith in the Holy Trinity.

THERE is but one living and true God, everlasting, without body, parts, or passions; of infinite power, wisdom, and goodness; the Maker, and Preserver of all things both visible and invisible. And in the unity of this Godhead there be three Persons, of one substance, power, and eternity; the Father, the Son, and the Holy Ghost.

II. Of the Word or Son of God, which was made very man.

THE Son, which is the Word of the Father, begotten from everlasting of the Father, the very and eternal God, and of one substance with the Father, took Man's nature in the womb of the blessed Virgin, of her substance: so that two whole and perfect Natures, that is to say, the Godhead and Manhood, were joined together in one Person, never to be divided, whereof is one Christ, very God, and very Man; who truly suffered, was crucified, dead, and buried, to reconcile his Father to us, and to be a sacrifice, not only for original guilt, but also for actual sins of men.

III. Of the going down of Christ into Hell.

AS Christ died for us, and was buried; so also it is to be believed, that he went down into Hell.

IV. Of the Resurrection of Christ.

CHRIST did truly rise again from death, and took again his body, with flesh, bones, and all things appertaining to the perfection of Man's nature; wherewith he ascended into Heaven, and there sitteth, until he return to judge all Men at the last day.

V. Of the Holy Ghost.

THE Holy Ghost, proceeding from the Father and the Son, is of one substance, majesty, and glory, with the Father and the Son, very and eternal God.

VI. Of the Sufficiency of the Holy Scriptures for Salvation.

HOLY Scripture containeth all things necessary to salvation: so that whatsoever is not read therein, nor may be proved thereby, is not to be required of any man, that it should be believed as an article of the Faith, or be thought requisite or necessary to salvation. In the name of the Holy Scripture we do understand those canonical Books of the Old and New Testament, of whose authority was never any doubt in the Church.

Of the Names and Number of the Canonical Books.

Genesis,	The First Book of Samuel	The Book of Ester,
Exodus	The Second Book of Samuel	The Book of Job,

Leviticus	The First Book of Kings	The Psalms,
Numbers	The Second Book of Kings	The Proverbs
Deuteronomy	The First Book of Chronicles	Ecclesiastes or Preacher,
Joshua	The Second Book of Chronicles	Cantica, or Songs of Solomon,
Judges	The First Book of Esdras	Four Prophets the greater,
Ruth	The Second Book of Esdras	Twelve Prophets the less.

And the other Books (as Hierome saith) the Church doth read for example of life and instruction of manners; but yet doth it not apply them to establish any doctrine; such are these following

The Third Book of Esdras,	The rest of the Book of Esther,
The Fourth Book of Esdras,	The Book of Wisdom,
The Book of Tobias,	Jesus the Son of Sirach,
The Book of Judith,	Baruch the Prophet,
The Song of the Three Children	The Prayet of Manasses
The Story of Susana,	The First Book of Maccabees,
Of Bel and the Dragon,	The Second Book of Maccabees.

All the Books of the New Testament, as they are commonly received, we do receive, and account them Canonical.

VII. Of the Old Testament.

THE Old Testament is not contrary to the New: for both in the Old and New Testament everlasting life is offered to Mankind by Christ, who is the only Mediator between God and Man, being both God and Man. Wherefore they are not to be heard, which feign that the old Fathers did look only for transitory promises. Although the Law given from God by Moses, as touching Ceremonies and Rites, do not bind Christian men, nor the Civil precepts thereof ought of necessity to be received in any commonwealth; yet notwithstanding, no Christian man whatsoever is free from the obedience of the Commandments which are called Moral.

VIII. Of the Creeds.

The Nicene Creed, and that which is commonly called the Apostles' Creed, ought thoroughly to be received and believed: for they may be proved by most certain warrants of Holy Scripture.

IX. Of Original or Birth-Sin.

ORIGINAL sin standeth not in the following of Adam, (as the Pelagians do vainly talk;) but it is the fault and corruption of the Nature of every man, that naturally is engendered of the offspring of Adam; whereby man is very far gone from original righteousness, and is of his own nature inclined to evil, so that the flesh lusteth always contrary to the Spirit; and therefore in every person born into this world, it deserveth God's wrath and damnation. And this infection of nature doth remain, yea in them that are regenerated; whereby the lust of the flesh, called in Greek, *fronhma sarkos*, (which some do expound the wisdom, some sensuality, some the affection, some the desire, of the flesh), is not subject to the Law of God. And although there is no condemnation for them that believe and are baptized; yet the Apostle doth confess, that concupiscence and lust hath of itself the nature of sin.

X. Of Free Will.

THE condition of Man after the fall of Adam is such, that he cannot turn and prepare himself, by his own natural strength and good works, to faith, and calling upon God. Wherefore we have no power to do good works pleasant and acceptable to God, without the grace of God by Christ preventing us, that we may have a good will, and working with us, when we have that good will.

XI. Of the Justification of Man.

WE are accounted righteous before God, only for the merit of our Lord and Saviour Jesus Christ by Faith, and not for our own works or deservings. Wherefore, that we are justified by Faith only, is a most wholesome Doctrine, and very full of comfort, as more largely is expressed in the Homily of Justification.

XII. Of Good Works.

ALBEIT that Good Works, which are the fruits of Faith, and follow after Justification, cannot put away our sins, and endure the severity of God's judgment; yet are they pleasing and acceptable to God in Christ, and do spring out necessarily of a true and lively Faith; insomuch that by them a lively Faith may be as evidently known as a tree discerned by the fruit.

XIII. Of Works before Justification.

WORKS done before the grace of Christ, and the Inspiration of the Spirit, are not pleasant to God, forasmuch as they spring not of faith in Jesus Christ; neither do they make men meet to receive grace, or (as the School-authors say) deserve grace of congruity: yea rather, for that they are not done as God hath willed and commanded them to be done, we doubt not but they have the nature of sin.

XIV. Of Works of Supererogation.

VOLUNTARY Works besides, over and above, God's Commandments, which they call Works of Supererogation, cannot be taught without arrogancy and impiety: for by them men do declare, that they do not only render unto God as much as they are bound to, but that they do more for his sake, than of bounden duty is required: whereas Christ saith plainly, When ye have done all that are commanded to you, say, We are unprofitable servants.

XV. Of Christ alone without Sin.

CHRIST in the truth of our nature was made like unto us in all things, sin only except, from which he was clearly void, both in his flesh, and in his spirit. He came to be the Lamb without spot, who, by sacrifice of himself once made, should take away the sins of the world; and sin (as Saint John saith) was not in him. But all we the rest, although baptized, and born again in Christ, yet offend in many things; and if we say we have no sin, we deceive ourselves, and the truth is not in us.

XVI. Of Sin after Baptism.

NOT every deadly sin willingly committed after Baptism is sin against the Holy Ghost, and unpardonable. Wherefore the grant of repentance is not to be denied to such as fall into sin after Baptism. After we have received the Holy Ghost, we may depart from grace given, and fall into sin, and by the grace of God we may arise again, and amend our lives. And therefore they are to be condemned, which say, they can no more sin as long as they live here, or deny the place of forgiveness to such as truly repent.

XVII. Of Predestination and Election.

PREDESTINATION to Life is the everlasting purpose of God, whereby (before the foundations of the world were laid) he hath constantly decreed by his counsel secret to us, to deliver from curse and damnation those whom he hath chosen in Christ out of mankind, and to bring them by Christ to ever- lasting salvation, as vessels made to honour. Wherefore, they which be endued with so excellent a benefit of God, be called according to God's purpose by his Spirit working in due season: they through Grace obey the calling: they be justified freely: they be made sons of God by adoption: they be made like the image of his only-begotten Son Jesus Christ: they walk religiously in good works, and at length, by God's mercy, they attain to everlasting felicity.

As the godly consideration of Predestination, and our Election in Christ, is full of sweet, pleasant, and unspeakable comfort to godly persons, and such as feel in themselves the working of the Spirit of Christ, mortifying the works of the flesh, and their earthly members, and drawing up their mind to high and heavenly things, as well because it doth greatly establish and confirm their faith of eternal Salvation to be enjoyed through Christ, as because it doth fervently kindle their love towards God: So, for curious and carnal persons, lacking the Spirit of Christ, to have continually before their eyes the sentence of God's Predestination, is a most dangerous downfall, whereby the Devil doth thrust them either into desperation, or into wretchlessness of most unclean living, no less perilous than desperation.

Furthermore, we must receive God's promises in such wise, as they be generally set forth to us in Holy Scripture: and, in our doings, that Will of God is to be followed, which we have expressly declared unto us in the word of God.

XVIII. Of obtaining eternal Salvation only by the Name of Christ.

THEY also are to be had accursed that presume to say, That every man shall be saved by the Law or Sect which he professeth, so that he be diligent to frame his life according to that Law, and the light of

Nature. For Holy Scripture doth set out unto us only the Name of Jesus Christ, whereby men must be saved.

XIX. Of the Church.

THE visible Church of Christ is a congregation of faithful men, in which the pure Word of God is preached, and the Sacraments be duly ministered according to Christ's ordinance, in all those things that of necessity are requisite to the same.

As the Church of Jerusalem, Alexandria, and Antioch, have erred; so also the Church of Rome hath erred, not only in their living and manner of Ceremonies, but also in matters of Faith.

XX. Of the Authority of the Church.

THE Church hath power to decree Rites or Ceremonies, and authority in Controversies of Faith: and yet it is not lawful for the Church to ordain anything that is contrary to God's Word written, neither may it so expound one place of Scripture, that it be repugnant to another. Wherefore, although the Church be a witness and a keeper of Holy Writ, yet, as it ought not to decree any thing against the same, so besides the same ought not to enforce any thing to be believed for necessity of Salvation.

XXI. Of the Authority of General Councils.

[The Twenty-first of the former Articles is omitted; because it is partly of a local and civil nature, and is provided for, as to the remaining parts of it, in other Articles.]

XXII. Of Purgatory.

THE Romish Doctrine concerning Purgatory, Pardons, Worshipping and Adoration, as well of Images as of Relics, and also Invocation of Saints, is a fond thing, vainly invented, and grounded upon no warranty of Scripture, but rather repugnant to the Word of God.

XXIII. Of Ministering in the Congregation.

IT is not lawful for any man to take upon him the office of public preaching, or ministering the Sacraments in the Congregation, before he be lawfully called, and sent to execute the same. And those we ought to judge lawfully called and sent, which be chosen and called to this work by men who have public authority given unto them in the Congregation, to call and send Ministers into the Lord's vineyard.

XXIV. Of Speaking in the Congregation in such a Tongue as the people understandeth.

IT is a thing plainly repugnant to the Word of God, and the custom of the Primitive Church, to have public Prayer in the Church, or to minister the

Sacraments, in a tongue not understanded of the people.

XXV. Of the Sacraments.

SACRAMENTS ordained of Christ be not only badges or tokens of Christian men's profession, but rather they be certain sure witnesses, and effectual signs of grace, and God's good will towards us, by the which he doth work invisibly in us, and doth not only quicken, but also strengthen and confirm our Faith in him.

There are two Sacraments ordained of Christ our Lord in the Gospel, that is to say, Baptism, and the Supper of the Lord.

Those five commonly called Sacraments, that is to say, Confirmation, Penance, Orders, Matrimony, and Extreme Unction, are not to be counted for Sacraments of the Gospel, being such as have grown partly of the corrupt following of the Apostles, partly are states of life allowed in the Scriptures; but yet have not like nature of Sacraments with Baptism, and the Lord's Sup- per, for that they have not any visible sign or ceremony ordained of God.

The Sacraments are not ordained of Christ to be gazed upon, or to be carried about, but that we should duly use them. And in such only as worthily receive the same, they have a wholesome effect or operation: but they that receive them unworthily, purchase to themselves damnation, as Saint Paul saith.

XXVI. Of the Unworthiness of the Ministers, which hinders not the effect of the Sacraments.

ALTHOUGH in the visible Church the evil be ever mingled with the good, and sometimes the evil have chief authority in the Ministration of the Word and Sacraments, yet forasmuch as they do not the same in their own name, but in Christ's, and do minister by his commission and authority, we may use their Ministry, both in hearing the Word of God, and in receiving the Sacraments. Neither is the effect of Christ's ordinance taken away by their wickedness, nor the grace of God's gifts diminished from such as by faith, and rightly, do receive the Sacraments ministered unto them; which be effectual, because of Christ's institution and promise, although they be ministered by evil men.

Nevertheless, it appertaineth to the discipline of the Church, that inquiry be made of evil Ministers, and that they be accused by those that have knowledge of their offences; and finally, being found guilty, by just judgment be deposed.

XXVII. Of Baptism.

BAPTISM is not only a sign of profession, and mark of difference, whereby Christian men are discerned from others that be not christened, but it is also a sign of Regeneration or New-Birth, whereby, as by an instrument, they that receive Baptism rightly are grafted into the Church; the promises of the forgiveness of sin, and of our adoption to be the sons of God by the Holy Ghost, are visibly signed and sealed; Faith is confirmed, and Grace increased by virtue of prayer unto God.

The Baptism of young Children is in any wise to be retained in the Church, as most agreeable with the institution of Christ.

XXVIII. Of the Lord's Supper.

THE Supper of the Lord is not only a sign of the love that Christians ought to have among themselves one to another; but rather it is a Sacrament of our Redemption by Christ's death: insomuch that to such as rightly, worthily, and with faith, receive the same, the Bread which we break is a partaking of the Body of Christ; and likewise the Cup of Blessing is a partaking of the Blood of Christ.

Transubstantiation (or the change of the substance of Bread and Wine) in the Supper of the Lord, cannot be proved by Holy Writ; but is repugnant to the plain words of Scripture, overthroweth the nature of a Sacrament, and hath given occasion to many superstitions.

The Body of Christ is given, taken, and eaten, in the Supper, only after an heavenly and spiritual manner.

And the mean whereby the Body of Christ is received and eaten in the Supper, is Faith.

The Sacrament of the Lord's Supper was not by Christ's ordinance reserved, carried about, lifted up, or worshipped.

XXIX. Of the Wicked, which eat not the Body of Christ in the use of the Lord's Supper.

THE Wicked, and such as be void of a lively faith, although they do carnally and visibly press with their teeth (as Saint Augustine saith) the Sacrament of the Body and Blood of Christ; yet in no wise are they partakers of Christ: but rather, to their condemnation, do eat and drink the sign or Sacrament of so great a thing.

XXX. Of both Kinds.

THE Cup of the Lord is not to be denied to the Lay-people: for both the parts of the Lord's Sacrament, by Christ's ordinance and commandment, ought to be ministered to all Christian men alike.

XXXI. Of the one Oblation of Christ finished upon the Cross.

THE Offering of Christ once made in that perfect redemption, propitiation, and satisfaction, for all the sins of the whole world, both original and actual;

and there is none other satisfaction for sin, but that alone. Wherefore the sacrifices of Masses, in the which it was commonly said, that the Priest did offer Christ for the quick and the dead, to have remission of pain or guilt, were blasphemous fables, and dangerous deceits.

XXXII. Of the Marriage of Priests.

Bishops, Priests, and Deacons, are not commanded by God's Law, either to vow the estate of single life, or to abstain from marriage: therefore it is lawful for them, as for all other Christian men, to marry at their own discretion, as they shall judge the same to serve better to godliness.

XXXIII. Of excommunicate Persons, how they are to be avoided.

THAT person which by open denunciation of the Church is rightly cut off from the unity of the Church, and excommunicated, ought to be taken of the whole multitude of the faithful, as an Heathen and Publican, until he be openly reconciled by penance, and received into the Church by a Judge that hath the authority thereunto.

XXXIV. Of the Traditions of the Church.

IT is not necessary that the Traditions and Ceremonies be in all places one, or utterly like; for at all times they have been divers, and may be changed according to the diversity of countries, times, and men's manners, so that nothing be ordained against God's Word. Whosoever, through his private judgment, willingly and purposely, doth openly break the Traditions and Ceremonies of the Church, which be not repugnant to the Word of God, and be ordained and approved by common authority, ought to be rebuked openly, (that others may fear to do the like,) as he that offendeth against the common order of the Church, and hurteth the authority of the Magistrate, and woundeth the consciences of the weak brethren.

Every particular or national Church hath authority to ordain, change, and abolish, Ceremonies or Rites of the Church ordained only by man's authority, so that all things be done to edifying.

XXXV. Of the Homilies.

THE Second Book of Homilies, the several titles whereof we have joined under this Article, doth contain a godly and wholesome Doctrine, and necessary for these times, as doth the former Book of Homilies, which were set forth in the time of Edward the Sixth; and therefore we judge them to be read in Churches by the Ministers, diligently and distinctly, that they may be understanded of the people.

Of the Names of the Homilies.

1 Of the right Use of the Church.
2 Against Peril of Idolatry.
3 Of repairing and keeping clean of Churches.
4 Of good Works: first of Fasting.
5 Against Gluttony and Drunkenness.
6 Against Excess of Apparel.

[This Article is received in this Church, so far as it declares the Book of Homilies to be an explication of Christian doctrine, and instructive in piety and m orals. But all references to the constitution and laws of England are considered as inapplicable to the circum- stances of this Church; which also suspends the order for the reading of said Homilies in churches, until a revision of them may be conveniently made, for the clearing of them, as well from obsolete words and phrases, as from the local references.]

XXXVI. Of Consecration of Bishops and Ministers.

THE Book of Consecration of Bishops, and Ordering of Priests and Deacons, as set forth by the General

Convention of this Church in 1792, doth contain all things necessary to such Consecration and Ordering; neither hath it any thing that, of itself, is superstitious and ungodly. And, therefore, whosoever are consecrated or ordered according to said Form, we decree all such to be rightly, orderly, and lawfully consecrated and ordered.

XXXVII. Of the Power of the Civil Magistrates.

THE Power of the Civil Magistrate extendeth to all men, as well Clergy as Laity, in all things temporal; but hath no authority in things purely spiritual. And we hold it to be the duty of all men who are professors of the Gospel, to pay respectful obedience to the Civil Authority, regularly and legitimately constituted.

XXXVIII. Of Christian Men's Goods, which are not common.

THE Riches and Goods of Christians are not common, as touching the right, title, and possession of the same; as certain Anabaptists do falsely boast. Notwithstanding, every man ought, of such things as he possesseth, liberally to give alms to the poor, according to his ability.

XXXIX. Of a Christian Man's Oath.

AS we confess that vain and rash Swearing is forbidden Christian men by our Lord Jesus Christ, and James his Apostle, so we judge, that Christian

Religion doth not prohibit, but that a man may swear when the Magistrate requireth, in a cause of faith and charity, so it be done according to the Prophet's teaching in justice, judgment, and truth.

Appendix F

Some Important and Possibly Interesting Events

A.D. 33 Jesus – "Go into all the world to make disciples" Matthew 28.

Late 2nd Century – Christians are now in Britain. Perhaps Roman soldiers were the first missionaries on English soil.

3rd Century – St Alban, Britain's first Christian martyr.

314 – Council of Arles. Three English bishops attend synod on the Continent, suggesting a well organized ecclesiastical structure in Britain.

596 – Pope Gregory of Rome sends Augustine to Britain.

664 – Council of Whitby. Roman Catholicism adopted officially in Britain. Before that the Celtic form of Christianity had prevailed.

1215 – Magna Carta limiting the power of English monarchs and guaranteeing that the English Church would be free.

1384 – John Wycliff, a professor at Oxford, (England's "first protestant") translates the Bible into English and calls for the church to return to the Bible and early church fathers.

14th and 15th Centuries – Renaissance revival in learning, art and literature.

1450 – Gutenberg Bible. First moveable-type printing makes Christian literature much more available.

16th Century – Growth of nationalism undermines papal authority, making Reformation inevitable.

1517 – Luther's *95 Theses* posted on Wittenberg Church door. Luther's writings influence scholars at Cambridge (White Horse Tavern).

1525 – William Tyndale translates Bible into English from the Greek and Hebrew scriptures.

1534 – King Henry VIII's Act of Supremacy, establishes the Church of England separate from Rome. Thomas Cranmer, Archbishop of Canterbury, authorizes and promotes the English Bible.

1539 –Six Articles. Although Henry breaks with Rome he retains Roman Catholic practices: transubstantiation, communion in one kind, permanent monastic vows, indulgences, mandatory confession to a priest, celibacy for clergy.

1549 – 1st Book of Common Prayer and major reforms under "the boy king" Edward VI. Cranmer leads Anglicanism more fully into Protestantism.

1553 – Roman Catholic Queen Mary seeks to re-Romanize England. Cranmer, Ridley, Latimer, Hooper burned at the stake.

1558 – Queen Elizabeth I commences 45 year reign bringing a broad comprehensiveness, fully Protestant once more but with squishy Catholic flavor.

1607 – Jamestown, Virginia, settlement of Anglicans some 16 years before Pilgrims arrive in Plymouth; no Anglican bishops for another 177 years, until Bishop Seabury.

1611 – Rev. Alex Whitaker, evangelical evangelist "Apostle to Virginia."

1730's to 1750's – Great Awakening led by George Whitefield (Jonathan Edwards) in America and John Wesley in England.

1776 – The Declaration of Independence. Revolution cuts the American branch of the Church of England off from England.

1784 – Samuel Seabury, Connecticut clergy choose him to be consecrated a bishop in Aberdeen, Scotland.

1785 – First General Convention of the Protestant Episcopal Church in Philadelphia.

1787 – American William White consecrated bishop at Lambeth Palace, England. Bicameral national church governance, with strong role for lay and clergy, central unit of ministry is local church, 39 Articles as our authority, reading list that influenced the next generation of those ordained.

1789 – 1st American Prayer Book and Constitution and Canons adopted.

1800 to1850 – Moral revival by evangelicals in England. William Wilberforce leads fight to abolish slavery 1830.

1801 – Authority of 39 Articles of Religion endorsed as the theological standard for the Episcopal Church.

1833 - Oxford Movement, Tracts for the Times (in England), seeks to return the church to pre-Reformation times.

1835-1893 - Philips Brooks, Bishop of Massachusetts, the Broad Church movement (Reduces the Bible to be the "story" of revelation, rather than revelation itself).

1842 – Nashotah House started in Wisconsin as ministry to Indian Tribes, evolves into seminary.

1860 – Reviews & Essays, seven highly influential essays by Church of England theologian that stated a higher critical view of Scripture.

1873 - The Reformed Episcopal Church formed in protest of "Romanism" in Episcopal Church, led by assistant bishop of Kentucky, George Cummins

1888 - Chicago-Lambeth Quadrilateral – A four-point articulation of Anglican Identity. [The Holy Scriptures, as containing all things necessary to salvation; The Creeds (specifically, the Apostles' and Nicene Creeds), as the sufficient statement of Christian faith; The Sacraments of Baptism and Holy Communion; The historic episcopate, locally adapted.]

1889 - "Lux mundi," Anglicans move from centrality of atonement to incarnation – A collection of essays intended to justify Christian faith in the light of contemporary thought.

1919 – A National Council of the Episcopal Church is organized to carry out the functions of the General Convention between triennial Conventions.

1928 – 3rd American Book of Common Prayer. (1st 1789, 2nd 1892).

1960 – With the help of Dennis Bennett's book *Nine O'clock in the Morning,* Episcopalians discover the power of the Holy Spirit.

1966 – Time Magazine features Paul van Buren (the Death of God, or Is God Dead?, movement).

1968 – Episcopal Church membership peaks at 4 million; somewhat less than half that today.

1974 – "Irregular" ordination of the "Philadelphia 11" women priests.

1976 – Trinity Episcopal School for Ministry founded in Ambridge, Pennslyvania.

1979 – 4th American Book of Common Prayer; emasculates the oath required of a Bishop.

1989 – Righter Trial of Barry Stopfel, determines the Episcopal Church has no doctrine related to sexual behavior.

1991 – George Carey elevated to Archbishop of Canterbury.

2000 - Chuck Murphy and John Rogers consecrated in Singapore as bishops for America, starting the Anglican Mission in North America (AMiA).

2002 – Rowan Williams elevated to Archbishop of Canterbury.

2003 – Episcopal General Convention consents to Gene Robinson as Bishop of New Hampshire, the first openly gay bishop, signaling the beginning of the realignment of Anglicans in America.

2003 – Plano, Texas (Dallas) Conference of orthodox Anglicans.

2003 to 2009 – Pending formation of an orthodox Anglican Church in North America congregations having left the Episcopal Church receive spiritual oversight from other members of the Anglican Communion (including the Anglican Churches of Argentina, Bolivia, Nigeria, Rwanda, and Uganda). Orthodox American Anglican groups coalesce in the Common Cause Partnership that evolves as the Anglican Church in North America.

2008 – Global Anglican Futures Conference (GAFCON) meets in Jerusalem. *The Jerusalem Declaration* endorses the formation of the Anglican Church in North America.

2008 – The Fellowship of Confessing Anglicans is formed to extend the goals of GAFCON.

2009 – The Anglican Church in North America (ACNA) is formed. The Rt. Rev. Bob Duncan is installed as Archbishop and Primate.

2013 – 2nd GAFCON in Nairobi, Kenya.

2013 to 2014 – The first portion of an eventual ACNA Prayer Book is published. *To Be A Christian*, ACNA's Catechism, is published.

June 2014 – The Rt. Rev. Foley Beach is elected the second Archbishop and Primate of ACNA.

October 2014 – Primates representing a majority of Anglicans worldwide lay hands on ACNA Archbishop Foley Beach to welcome him into the Anglican Communion as an Archbishop and Primate.